Armey's Axioms

*40 Hard-Earned
Truths from Politics,
Faith, and Life*

Dick Armey

John Wiley & Sons, Inc.

Published by John Wiley & Sons, Inc., Hoboken, New Jersey
Published simultaneously in Canada

Design and production by Navta Associates, Inc.

For general information about our other products and services, please contact our Customer Care Department within the United States at (800) 762-2974, outside the United States at (317) 572-3993 or fax (317) 572-4002.

Wiley also publishes its books in a variety of electronic formats. Some content that appears in print may not be available in electronic books. For more information about Wiley products, visit our web site at www.wiley.com.

ISBN 0-471-46913-0

Printed in the United States of America

10 9 8 7 6 5 4 3 2 1

In loving memory of
Marion and Glenn F. Armey

CONTENTS

CONTENTS

CONTENTS

CONTENTS

FOREWORD

I suppose I am just one of a great many people who have
found both enlightenment and amusement in Dick Armey's
axioms over the years. I know I am one person who encouraged him to write them down and publish them. Now that I
have read this book, I am glad he took my advice. Still, there
are a couple of Armey's Axioms that I might rather have been
left out. But that is the beauty of the book. For many of us,
most of the axioms will be entertaining, encouraging, and
insightful. But each of us who reads this book will see something of ourselves that might need a bit of correction. I suppose everyone can benefit from reading a book that makes us
a bit uncomfortable from time to time.

Dick Armey manages to take some of the most difficult
issues of public policy, economics, and theology and present
them in a lighthearted, humorous style. It is so like him to
give us humor with relevance in a down-home, plainspoken
manner. Just when we begin to feel too bogged down in difficult and serious discussions, he throws in marathon running
and quarter horses. We all take ourselves oh so seriously that

we forget that some of life's most important lessons can be found in everyday events, challenges, and crises. All we need to do is take a deep breath and open our eyes to what's going on around us, and we will be the better for it. That's the nub of what Dick teaches us.

While he tends to be a private man, this book gives some insight into his personal life. He seems to be especially open when professing his love of the Lord and his family. Yet, he doesn't overwhelm us with personal details, but sticks to telling us about what works for him and inviting us to try it for ourselves. There's much to learn in this book for people from all walks of life and of all faiths. Find a nice comfy chair and enjoy.

—Sean Hannity

PREFACE

As a professor of economics many years ago, I tried to find a way to capture complex ideas in short, memorable notions. I adopted the convention of "Armey's Axioms." This was designed to catch the student's imagination and to give him an amusing handle on difficult ideas. For example, "Armey's Axiom number one: The market's rational, the government's dumb" had a catchy alliteration and was the predicate for an entire graduate seminar in public choice theory. Since the course was esoteric and difficult, you will be spared from it in this book. However, many of the axioms found in the book were first derived in that course. The approach worked for the students and they enjoyed the axioms so I accumulated quite a few over the years and I shared them generously until they became a natural and expected part of my discussions.

Once I became a member of Congress and later the majority leader, my axioms seemed to get much more notice. I was pleased when other people quoted them. Furthermore, people began to urge me to write them down and put them in a book. Consequently, I began compiling the collection in anticipation of my retirement from Congress. I am now retired, and here they are. Most of them are original with me. Some are borrowed, I regret, from forgotten sources. Wherever possible I have tried to give thanks to those who inspired the axiom. Where I have failed to remember the appropriate acknowledgment, I sincerely apologize.

This book was written primarily for the fun of it, and I hope it will be read for the same reason. Still, the reader may find some worthwhile lessons tucked away in some of the chapters. I have tried to relate each axiom to some event in my life, and I invite readers to do the same for theirs. I want to thank John Wiley & Sons for publishing the book, especially Kitt Alan, my publisher, and even more especially Hana Lane, my editor. Hana is a delightful person and generously professional. She seemed to catch the spirit of what I was trying to do and supported it with much insight, encouragement, and, when necessary, discipline. I would hate to think what this effort would be without her. Her insistence on brevity may have saved the project from being excruciatingly boring. Hana taught me that the word "that" is a good word and that there is no reason on God's green earth to use a semicolon. John Simko did a fine job of coordinating the book's production and keeping me on schedule. Alexa Selph did a marvelous job of copyediting and taught me not to subcontract my punctuation to a diarrhetic fly.

I want to thank my wife, Susan, who painstakingly read every word. Her insights were many and did much to improve the book. I can't tell how many times she saved me from my inner child, with whom I consort far too much. Likewise, I thank Alyne, Betsy, and Ryan Byrd for their many helpful suggestions. Bill and Sherri Detwiler and Ken and Lou Ann Rogers also read the manuscript and offered good advice and encouragement. Our children and parents, along with many associates over the years, inspired much of what is written here. Susan and I are proud of our five children and their spouses. We hope they enjoy this book and can find use of it in raising our grandchildren who bring such joy to our lives.

I want to thank Sean Hannity for his fine foreword. He is a good friend and generous to contribute. Finally, I want to thank the reader for buying the book. As in every good market transaction, now we can both profit.

Freedom
works

*We hold these Truths to be self-evident, that all Men are
created equal, that they are endowed by their Creator
with certain unalienable Rights, that among these are
Life, Liberty, and the Pursuit of Happiness.*

—THE DECLARATION OF INDEPENDENCE

I t is no wonder that everyone cherishes freedom. On some
level, we all understand freedom to be our natural condi-
tion. Still, in fact, none of us is wholly free, for we are all
answerable to God in the end. As our founding fathers said, it
is God who gives us freedom in this, our mortal, life. Indeed,
the two characteristics that distinguish mankind from all other
creatures are intelligence and freedom. Only man has the
ability to understand the wonders of the universe and the
ability to alter it for his own comfort. No animal can do this.
God, the creator, made man in His own image by endowing
him with creativity. Not the power to create, for God holds
that for Himself, but the power to understand and to alter
God's creations to his comfort. That is freedom, and freedom
works.

Freedom is not license. Freedom is not free. True freedom carries with it responsibility and accountability. Unfortunately, this is not always understood. Some people don't feel
free unless they are free *from* responsibility. If that is your

understanding, you will never be free, and you will never be happy. You will live your life like a hapless child being forever a victim in a world that seems too demanding and too cruel. You will miss your chance to be a success in your own life and a joy in the lives of others, for that false freedom that we call license does not work. It does not work because it is incomplete. God did not give you freedom "no strings attached" because He knew the harm you would do with it. No, His gift was the right to be your own person with the constraint of accountability first to others in this life and then ultimately for all eternity to Holy God Almighty Himself. It is from that accountability that we learn lessons of responsibility.

It is not only in the lives of individuals that freedom works, but also in the fate of nations. Nation-states can be organized along vertical lines of power, control, and submission to a central authority or along horizontal lines of respect and voluntary association. For simplicity's sake, let's call the former authoritarian states and the latter democracies. The essential difference is in respect for the rights of others to live as the free men and women God intended them to be. While power and dominion over others may work well, at least in the short run, for those who hold it, it does not work well for those who are subjugated to it. Freedom, on the other hand, works for everyone.

Consider East and West Germany, North and South Korea, the People's Republic of China and the Republic of China (Taiwan), and the People's Republic of China and Hong Kong. In each case you find people of the same cultural heritage, some living with tyranny and others living free. In each case the victims of tyranny are worse off in every dimension of life: economic, social, political, spiritual, and emotional. Every measurable observation about "quality of life" favors those who live free. Furthermore, just as the history of immigration patterns has demonstrated the desire to flee totalitarian states for freedom, the history of nation-states has been to reject tyranny for freedom. Witness, for example, the American Revolution, the French Revolution, the breakup of the Soviet Empire, and the fall of the Berlin Wall.

Tyrants have always denied freedom of religion, a freedom that subjugated people inevitably hunger for. Why? Because tyrants have known what people know: Truth is ultimately found in Holy Scripture and the truth will set you free. When people know that God intended them to be free in this life, they demand that freedom. This is never so clear as in Christianity, where people draw courage from their Lord Jesus Christ, who freely fulfilled His responsibility and our accountability on the cross so we can be free as God intended. It is no wonder that the enemies of freedom are the enemies of religion. It is no wonder that lovers of freedom ground that love in faith. For in faith, as with all things, freedom is possible. While the Lord God Almighty has the power to chain us to Him, He has the love and the respect to allow us to come of our own free will. We can honor our God and our Creator if we will do the same for one another. That is the duty of governments.

Freedom is our natural state, if we can hold on to it. Try as he might, no man can deny another his freedom. We can, however, forsake our freedom if we are weak. Just as Michael had to fight through Satan's demons to get to Daniel in order to interpret his dream correctly, we must with the Lord's help fight the demons of sophistry, pride, audacity, irresponsibility, unaccountability, tyranny, and fear to know our dream and keep our freedom. The fight is worth it because freedom is our greatest gift from God, and freedom works.

Armey's Axiom
Number 2

———————— ⚜ ————————

Macho
hurts

———————— ⚘ ————————

We men are funny. We seem to have an unlimited need to prove our manhood. We live lives inspired by manly sloganeering. Comments like "No pain, no gain" light us up. We are high-energy people, and we must have manly activities to burn off all our energy. It must be the testosterone. Maybe it's "he-man macho psychosis." All that is well and good except for our tendency to overdo things and hurt ourselves. We have this uncontrollable urge to be macho, and macho hurts.

Sooner or later we all come to this realization. For me it was during that brief time in my life when I ran seven marathons. To run a marathon is no small task. It takes months of training during which one runs at least seventy miles a week and, if one is smart, spends an hour a day in the weight room. My first marathon took four and a half hours. I ran it on the sea wall in Galveston, Texas. Most of it was run into a cold, wet wind off the gulf coast, and when I finished, even my hair hurt. During that race I observed a man running in his bare feet. How crazy is that? I once saw a man run a marathon in cowboy boots. How crazy is that? My second marathon was run in Lake Charles, Louisiana, in October. In that one, I decided early not to stop for water at any of the aid stations. How crazy is that? I literally crawled over the finish line four and a half hours later completely dehydrated and ready to die. But I finished, and when it comes to marathons, if you finish, you win. My third marathon was the White Rock Marathon in Dallas, Texas. That time I started at the head of the pack with all the young speedsters, and they ran me out in the first five miles. What had come over me? What possessed me to think I could keep up with Kenyans and Olympians? Since "The Rock" was two laps around the lake, it was very pleasant. Just as I was completing the first lap and approaching the finish line, I sensed an air of excitement in the crowd. They broke out in wildly enthusiastic cheers. I thought, "Boy, these people must love me." I felt a breeze and watched the winner zip past me. I actually saw him finish. Two hours later I finished to a hushed crowd that included few people not in my immediate family. But, I had beaten a seventy-year-old man. I guess he wasn't looking for a rematch!

My fourth marathon was the first ever Cowtown Marathon in Fort Worth, Texas. We ran that one on a cold, rainy day with snow and ice on the course. By that time I had come to the realization that I did not need to start up front with the Kenyans. I started further back and paced myself. I knew it was going better because I did not start to cry until about mile eighteen. Still, all my friends had run off and left me and I felt alone. By mile twenty-three I was dragging bad. I wanted to quit, but heck, anyone can stand anything for three miles. Just when I felt lower than a snake's belly, someone ran past me carrying a small radio. It was playing Tanya Tucker singing "Texas When I Die." It picked me up, and I kept up until the song was over. Then it started playing Waylon Jennings's "Slow Moving Outlaws." I fit right in with that.

I ran Cowtown one more time, and then I ran The Rock two more times. My times got better. By the time I ran my last marathon I did not cry until it was over, and I finished it in three hours and eighteen minutes. I started so far back that it took me over ten minutes to get to the starting line. I never saw a Kenyan or an Olympian. I ran ten miles with a girls' cross-country team and then went off and left them. They were more fun than the Kenyans. I did not have trouble with the first twenty-six miles, but that last 365 yards darn near killed me. I think it would be better to put those extra yards at the front of the race when the runners are still fresh. That was my last marathon. I am glad I ran them. I learned a lot from the experience, but most of all I learned that macho hurts. So today I fish. But, I still have not left my macho behind.

I recently had a tooth that began to hurt. I had no time for it. Over the weekend it got worse. I was sure it would get better. By Monday it was fairly painful, and my wife suggested that she call my dentist. I didn't need to fool with it. She persisted until I was forced to remember Jesse Ventura's memorable line from the movie *Predator*: "I don't have time to bleed!" That should have settled it, but my wife just smiled and reminded me, "Sometimes it is better to take time, Mr. Macho Man." By midnight I was writhing in pain with a face swollen larger than my macho ego and imploring my wife to call my dentist. She pointed out that she was not going to wake that good man in the middle of the night just because of my macho-maniacal delirium.

By morning she took pity on me and took me to the dentist, where he treated my abscessed tooth and put me on antibiotics so that I could spend the rest of the week recovering from a root canal and pondering how much less pain I would have had to endure if I had taken "time to bleed" on Monday. Still, it turned out better for me than for Jesse in the movie. He was killed, you know. Not only does macho hurt, but also, in the extreme, it can kill.

Armey's Axiom
Number 3

Tattoos last forever

W hen I was a boy, we had a crew on the place to dig a basement under our house. It was quite exciting. The house was on jacks, and the crew was digging out the basement by hand. I was fascinated with one man's right arm. That man was Curt Quackenbush. He had a hula girl tattooed over his muscle in such a way that she would dance as he flexed it. As a ten-year-old, I wanted one just like it. Curt told me to never get a tattoo, because they last forever. He was sorry he had ever done so. Later, my oldest brother went into the navy and came home with several tattoos. I thought they were neat until my father pointed out that, had his son been born with a birthmark, he would have spent thousands of dollars to have it removed for him. That settled the issue for me. If my father was against tattoos, they had to be wrong. I have been against them ever since.

We all have dominion over our own bodies so, literally, we don't have to have tattoos. But, figuratively, we can get them from "tattoo artists" who are beyond our control. I'm talking about the bum raps that people place on us in the form of allegations that are untrue or unfair. They are the unearned "scarlet letter" that reflects someone's label given to us for reasons of their own. Like physical tattoos, they last a lifetime, and we carry them to our graves. They will show up in our obituary for our children and grandchildren to read, and they will be a lasting part of our legacy not because they were true but because someone else wanted to keep them alive.

Any one of us can get these tattoos at any time. We may acquire them in the family, at work, in church, or in the community. We don't even understand why we get them in many cases, but we all get them. The question is, how are we supposed to live with them? Kris Kristofferson gives a good suggestion in a song he wrote about his father's advice to him. His father told him that when people do you wrong, you'll feel better if you take it like a man. How do you "take it like a man"? Put it in perspective. Your friends will always believe it is not true, and your enemies will always believe it is true. Cherish your friends, and as for your enemies, leave them to the Lord.

When we do things that are wrong, we should take the rap for them. We should do so with a certain amount of humility. But when the raps we take are untrue, we want them removed from our record just as we would want a tattoo removed from our arm. Unfortunately, that rarely happens. So, we must learn to live with it.

My friend Clarence Thomas has a tattoo given to him out of spite from people who did not like his legal philosophy and his political orientation. It is wrong and it should be removed. Clarence and I have talked about our "tattoos," and we know that they will be with us forever, but that doesn't make it right. Still, we know the scars we bear from false witnesses are not so severe and the price we pay is not so great as what was borne and paid for us by our Lord and Savior so we try to "take it like a man."

Armey's Axiom
Number 4

You can't stand on principle with feet of clay

We all like to think of ourselves as principled people. We like to think that we have fundamental core beliefs that are not compromised in what we do or say. When we commit to principles, we gain both responsibility and advantage. The responsibility is to stand for those principles and oftentimes to defend them. The advantage is that they give us a last refuge of rationale for the positions we take. When we hold fast to a position and seem to be stubborn and unreasonable, it is often convenient to explain, "I would like to be more helpful, but it is a matter of principle with me." This can be, and often is, an effective shield against retaliatory responses from those whom we disappoint. I remember a committee chairman refusing to include a particular provision in tax law because he opposed it on principle. The argument was going well for him and I was feeling guilty for challenging him until a friend pointed to the exact same provision in his last bill which he had included for his constituents. Oops, feet of clay. There are always those who will check on your "principled stands."

Speaker Dennis Hastert spent a good deal of time as the chief deputy whip for House Republicans. He took great pride in his ability to "get the tough votes." It was his job to obtain the necessary votes to pass bills on the floor of the House. With a thin and diverse majority, that was often a challenge and Denny used many techniques. He cajoled, traded, persuaded, threatened, demanded, encouraged, and, only when necessary, intimidated. We used to watch him work, and we enjoyed his high level of commitment and the pride he took in the fact that we rarely failed to get our votes. Denny made saying no a hard thing to do. My line on Denny was that the only part of the word no he understood was the part where he was saying it.

Somewhere along the way, Denny earned the nickname "teddy bear." He is a big man and an imposing figure, but he is a gentle soul. His effectiveness is born largely from his kindness, his consideration, and the professional respect he commands for his own, substantial, legislative abilities. Congressional folklore is that Dennis Hastert could not be denied because he twisted arms. But, that is simply not the case. Denny can be insistent, but he is a reasonable and considerate person. That is why, in its most troubled time, the House Republican majority turned to Dennis Hastert and elected him Speaker. Never before in all my life's experience did I see just the right person show up at just the right time and say, "I will serve." The nation is lucky to have him!

Denny understands and accepts the Republican ethos that nobody should be required to cast a vote in violation of his principles. The difference between Dennis Hastert and many others is he does not think that a principle is a sometimes thing. If a House member claims his vote as a matter of principle, he had better be able to demonstrate that he has always held to that principle and he had better not violate it sometime in the future. If he does, Denny will remember it and call him on it. I think that's fair enough. No one should expect another to believe that he is a person of conviction while he is drinking "backsliders wine." If it is a matter of principle, it can't be a matter of convenience.

Standing on principle is a serious business to be used sparingly. We had one House member who was always "standing on principle." In truth, he was often confused, indecisive, and lacking in courage. He did not like to be pressured by the leadership for his vote so he would claim every vote to be a matter of principle and scurry off the floor. When it came time for him to expect a subcommittee chairmanship by virtue of his tenure in the House, he did not get one. He was upset, but then he had never been available for the team when things were tough. He was naïve to expect the team to give him a leadership role when he couldn't find the courage to follow. Watching him waffle and quake while constantly shielding himself from the ordinary responsibilities of the job by making every inconvenient vote a matter of principle prompted me to create another Armey's Axiom: "If you are always standing on principle, you are going nowhere."

———— ⚜ ————

You can't get ahead while you're getting even

———— ⚜ ————

The conventional wisdom among many "sophisticated" people is to be coy and vengeful at the same time. They never let others see an honest expression of anger but instead contrive to take revenge at some later, more opportune, time. The idea is to inflict as much harm as possible and to do so by letting the moment of anger pass and hitting your adversaries later, when they least expect it. Rather than an honest confrontation that might resolve the matter, it is considered more savvy to become a master of the "sucker punch." These petty sophisticates exemplify the popular expression: "Don't get mad, get even." The result of this kind of thinking is to turn attention, time, and resources away from responsible behavior and to petty, spiteful, vindictiveness. This should seem a mighty small way for accomplished people to behave. Unfortunately, it is all too often taken as a sign of sophistication and shrewdness.

People can be careless, often thoughtless, frequently insensitive, and sometimes even downright rude or cruel.

Who among us has not been one or all of these at different moments in our lives? Why then should any of us feel free to respond to every little slight, every oversight, and every insult, with vengeance? It is because we are small, self-righteous, and self-indulgent. These characteristics are sometimes found in people who hold high office. In fact, the extraordinary deference paid to high office tends to encourage exactly those personality traits. That is why we often find vindictive people in high positions who do not overcrowd the high road of humility but, instead, wreak havoc on others while getting even. The irksome thing about the adage "Don't get mad, get even" is that it represents a vice as if it were a virtue. Pettiness appears to be sage. Thus, it sets a bad example for the uninitiated.

A better model is "You can't get ahead while you're getting even." What is your life all about? Is it about you, or some person or purpose outside you? If it is about yourself, you had better reconsider because, in the end, it will be no joy to you or anyone else. If it is about someone or some purpose outside yourself, you have more important things to consider than personal slights or insults. This point was made clearly one Sunday morning when, after church services, I, as the majority leader of the U.S. House, was being fussed over by some of the parishioners. When I was introduced to the elder Mother Camp, she said: "You know, young man, it isn't about you. It's about Jesus." If you want to get ahead, let it be about Jesus. If you haven't the faith for that, let it be about anything other than yourself. Have some self-respect. Have some dignity. Don't waste a position of trust on yourself. Serve out that trust for others and focus on commitments and objectives. Then you have a chance to be a success in your own life and a joy in the lives of others. If you need to get even, you might as well forget getting ahead. You will be so obsessed with past slights and so preoccupied with revenge that you will miss seeing the opportunities that lie ahead.

Consider the difference between looking back on your life and counting the number of people about whom you can say, "I sure showed them," or the number about whom you can say, "I showed them the way." Consider how much it matters in those lives, to them or to you. As they say in Texas: "This ain't no thinking thing." You know the right answer. The choice is yours. You can remain a child and struggle to get even, or you can be an adult and get ahead.

Armey's Axiom
Number 6

───────── ⚘ ─────────

If you love peace more than freedom, you lose

───────── ⚘ ─────────

Our love for peace is one of our most decent and honorable characteristics. It is also one of our most dangerous traits. There is probably nothing of greater comfort to despots than the love of peace when it is greater than the love of freedom. Churchill understood this. Chamberlain did not. Despots, of course, love having power and dominion over the lives of others. People who love freedom first will risk their peace to resist despotism in defense of their liberty. People who love peace first will risk both their peace and their freedom in vain attempts to appease despots. In the end, it is either the love of freedom or despotism that will prevail. With freedom, peace is possible. With despotism, servitude is inevitable. That is as true for individual relationships as it is for relationships between nations.

No matter what the relationship, whether it's within a family, social, professional, or among nations, it is impossible to appease people who hunger for power and control. People with a lust for power inevitably see appeasement as submission and are, thereby, encouraged to pursue an ever-increasing desire to control. People who meet aggression with compliance send the message "Go ahead and walk on me." This is the first playground lesson for most young people. Either the bully will encounter submission, in which case he perseveres, or he will meet resistance and learn to have some respect. Respect, after all, is what it is all about.

The love of power is about a lack of respect. In despotism there is always an underlying presumption of moral, intellectual, social, national, or racial superiority. Likewise, there is always a tacit presumption of inferiority or a lack of self-respect in acquiescence. In either case, it is a lack of respect for God and His creation. It is given to us in the Ten Commandments and in the Beatitudes to respect our fellow man and, as well, ourselves. Even as we must submit to legitimate authority, we must resist servitude. America has an extraordinary record in the love of freedom and peace, in that order. In fact, Americans have loved freedom so much they have often risked their peace for the freedom of others. That is the tradition we should preserve and the behavior we should emulate in our individual lives as well as in our national foreign policy.

While it is sometimes necessary to meet force with force, we should not meet aggression with aggression. Assertiveness and resolve are the answers. We need to know our boundaries and require that they be respected while we respect those of others. John Wayne said it well in the movie *The Shootist* when he said to Ron Howard, "I won't be wronged, I won't be lied to, and I won't be laid a hand on. *I do this for others* and I require the same for myself." It is a code of honor, and honor is a gift a man gives to himself. If you have it, others will know it and respect it.

If you love freedom, dignity, and respect and if you have the decency to love it for others as well, you can have peace. If you love power and have a need to control others, you will never have peace or freedom. If you fear power and submit to it, you will never have peace or freedom. The price of liberty in every aspect of our lives is eternal vigilance. That vigilance need not be belligerent, but it must be constant.

———————— ⚜ ————————

If you demagogue it, you own it

———————— ⚜ ————————

D emagoguery is the use of hyperbole and misinformation for political advantage by exaggerating either one's own virtue or the villainy of others. It is impossible for elected officials to completely separate their public responsibilities from their political interests. Even the most professional public officeholders wrestle with this conflict. Consequently, every public policy discussion is part policy and part politics. Successful demagoguery is shamelessly self-serving and irresponsible, a manifestation of the triumph of politics over policy. It is also a common practice in public policy discourse, because it works. Demagoguery, when done well, can give a person or a party an almost permanent and insurmountable advantage with some constituencies over some issues. That is why the art of demagoguery is so widely practiced by politicians.

Political stereotypes are the natural consequence of effective, long-term, consistent demagoguery. It is "the big lie," which if told long enough with a large enough "echo chamber," becomes the perception of reality and is not easily overcome. A good demagogue knows that to be effective he must get a good "buy in" by others who will be heard. In that way, when he lies, others will swear to it and the line can be sold and even established. Good demagogues cultivate and nurture their echo chambers. They often spin the story through the echo chamber first, see if it will fly, and then repeat it as if it originated from an "objective" source. It may be shameless, but it works.

In American politics, Democrats tend to be better demagogues than Republicans. The reason Democrats have more success at demagoguery is that they are more often liberal in their thinking than Republicans. Liberals are emotive and flexible with the facts. Hard facts and eternal truths are no friends of demagoguery. Flexibility and creativity are the keys to success. The idea is not to inform and help people but to "spin" them to your advantage. "Spin," it should be noted, is "substance abuse" and self-serving.

The greatest success in the practice of demagoguery in the American experience has been by the Democrats on the subject of Social Security. In 1964 the Democrats discovered the issue of Social Security as an instrument of their political success. During the presidential campaign of that year, Republican candidate Barry Goldwater thought it was time to look ahead and plan for inevitable problems in Social Security. Senator Goldwater was a serious man with serious public policy concerns. He knew that there was a disparity between future benefits and projected revenues. Given the large number of baby boomers, Social Security was not sustainable. He thought we should have a serious, forward-looking policy debate on the matter, and he set out, in his campaign, to do so. Lyndon Johnson would have none of that. He roared back, claiming Social Security to be a Democrat program and the most successful in the history of the world. He and he alone, he argued, would save the nation's elderly from Goldwater's secret scheme to "abolish Social Security." It worked. The echo chamber reverberated, and the message went out that "no serious discussion of Social Security will be tolerated." Poor Goldwater and the Republicans, they never knew what hit them.

The campaign of 1964 set the stage for the rest of the century. The stereotypes were sold. Democrats were the creators and defenders of Social Security. Social Security was the most successful program in the history of American public policy, and it had no problems—past, current, nor future. Republicans were mean-spirited people with a dislike for the elderly and secret plans to abolish Social Security. Over the years it seemed that any comment about Social Security from a Republican, no matter how benign, was interpreted as a secret plan to abolish the program. Republicans became so shell-shocked that they dubbed Social Security the "third rail of American politics"—"Touch it and you will die." Even in the late 1990s, when the whole world understood that Social Security was insolvent and lacked long-term viability, this legacy of successful demagoguery set the terms for national discourse on the subject.

By the end of the century everyone wanted Social Security fixed, but no one was willing to do it. Prudent Republicans knew they must control their natural policy impulses or risk political death for their party. If they took the lead on policy, they knew from experience that Democrats would revert to politics and wreak havoc on them. It is not prudent to put oneself at political risk against slim odds of achieving a policy success. So Republicans demurred. Democrats, on the other hand, would take no policy initiative because they wanted to continue with Social Security as a political issue. And so, we are at an impasse on the greatest public policy

issue and opportunity of our lifetime. The way to break the
impasse is for the Democrats to understand that since they
demagogue it, they own it. When they take the policy initiative, Republicans will work with them, and some great things
can happen as a result. The only other recourse is for the public to stand up at the ballot box on Election Day and say, "We
aren't falling for that anymore." It is true that "time wounds all
heels," and sooner or later the truth will catch up to even the
most adept and dedicated demagogue.

Successful demagoguery locks up policy until the demagogues decide to give up the political issue they have made
of it and accept their policy responsibilities. The reason is simple. Whether motivated by greed or fear, politics trumps policy. While politicians often give lip service to the better angels
of their nature, they rarely give public service to them and
they never trust their careers to them. In addition to Social
Security and Medicare, the Democrats have had other
remarkable demagogic successes, resulting in serious policy
impasses. One that comes quickly to mind is the excess of the
Environmental Protection Agency.

Democrats have had similar results with civil rights, labor
law, welfare, health care, education, and child care. In each case
they have had heartfelt programs and they developed large
echo chambers that gave them "public credibility." Each issue
is dangerous ground on which Republicans tread at their peril,
for they have little standing. The Republicans, on the other
hand, own anticommunism, family values, national defense,
antidrug programs, crime, and tax relief. The big difference
between Republicans and Democrats is that Republicans
don't want to own an issue for political advantage. Instead,
when they feel ownership, they want to make policy and get
it done. They have no heart for the "smart" political strategy of
holding back on policy in order to save it for their politics.

———————— ⚜ ————————

You can't get your finger on the problem if you've got it to the wind

———————— ⚜ ————————

P eople approach problems in two ways. Doers make decisions, and wafflers put their fingers to the wind. The difference between them is focus. Doers focus on the problem, ask for relevant information, look for the solution, and make up their minds. They get beyond themselves to what the problem is really about. They may be impulsive or they may be painstaking, but they get to a conclusion and they do something. Their concern is about how their decisions and actions address the problem at hand. They get their finger on the problem and focus on it rather than on themselves. Wafflers, on the other hand, keep the focus on themselves. Their concern is "what might happen to me as a result of the decision I make or the action I take." They can't get their finger on the problem because they have it to the wind.

The principal determinant of whether a person is a doer or a waffler is the strength of his conviction and his self-confidence. The same person might be decisive in one context and waffle in another. People tend to be more decisive when dealing with problems that fall into an area where they have expertise and a clear responsibility. They tend to be deferential in areas where they feel less qualified. They also tend to yield to social or professional position. This can take strange turns. For example, in some things Speaker trumps majority leader; in others wife trumps Speaker. Every once in a while, majority leader trumps Speaker, and even, on occasion, he trumps wife. There is a big difference between yielding to higher expertise or position and playing up to it. It is the difference between professionalism and sycophancy.

A strong leader will have no patience with sycophancy, and a strong person will not engage in it. A healthy, productive, decision-making relationship requires the ability to discern the differences among statements like the following:

Yes sir, you're the boss.	I think you're wrong, but you're the boss.
I don't know, what do you think?	You know more about that than me, what do you think?
What do the polls show?	What will people think?
Who benefits or is harmed?	What's in it for me?

Wafflers find many ways to avoid making a decision. Perhaps the most frustrating is paralysis by analysis. We all know the person who just can't get done thinking about it, analyzing it, and reworking it. These people know the devil is in the details, and they will not rest until they have covered every jot and tittle, crossed every t and dotted every i, and ferreted him out of there. They never get it done, but they are always busy working on it. A good leader gets rid of these compulsive perfectionists, sends them back to finish their thesis, or assigns them to busywork of little consequence. Still, they can be useful. If something comes up that needs attention but is better left unresolved, give it to the compulsive perfectionist.

Another common ploy in decision avoidance is to agree with everyone. How can anyone be faulted for being respectful and considerate? It also leaves one unaccountable. This is fine for someone not in charge who accepts that he likely never will be. It is downright dysfunctional for someone who is responsible for decisions getting made. You can't make a decision or make a friend if you are afraid of making an enemy. You can, however, assure that only the most recalcitrant person is well served by the outcome.

It is also useful in the pursuit of indecisiveness to know too much about the subject, its background and relevance. That allows you to talk about it until everyone is so tired they simply move on to new business. In that way, events can overtake you, and how things turn out will not be your fault. After all, you were working on it. It also impresses everyone with how brilliant you are. Glibness masquerading as brilliance results in a lot of credit given to people who make few decisions, and even fewer good decisions. This is especially true in government, where the consequences fall on others and are hard to document.

Often people don't make decisions because they don't like their choices. When we must choose between a good and a bad alternative, it is easy. Unhappily, that is rarely the case. Often the choice is among several good alternatives, and the decision must be based on which is "most best." Other times the choice is among several bad alternatives, and the decision must be based on what is the "least worst." These are difficult.

But, it can get worse. Hopefully one is looking for the "most best" or the "least worst" way to do the right thing. Sometimes we struggle with what is the "most best" or "least worst" way to keep the wrong thing from happening. We even struggle at times with what is the "least worst" or "most best" way to do the wrong thing. According to Waylon Jennings, There ain't no right way to do the wrong thing. Sometimes the right decision is to do nothing.

Finally, wafflers like to postpone things. Like Scarlett O'Hara, they'll think about that tomorrow. It's like driving a truck full of land mines down the road fearful they may explode and throwing them out in front of the truck to cover your rear. That doesn't fix the problem. It only assures that it will blow up in your face. Still, it feels like you are getting down the road, and there is always a chance they may not explode or will explode in someone else's face. Punt, that's the ticket. Never mind that the problem may end up in someone else's hands, it is out of yours, at least for now. That may be good enough for wafflers, but it is not good enough for doers. They know that the breeze on that finger in the wind is really a gale of discontent.

———————— ⚜ ————————

The politics of greed is wrapped in the language of love

———————— ⚜ ————————

It took Lyndon Johnson's guile, the Kennedy style, and the gullibility of the 1960s to establish a winning political formula for the Democrat party in the second half of the twentieth century. That formula can be summed up as the politics of greed wrapped in the language of love. It is built on the old political observation "If you can fake sincerity, you can win elections."

It was a good act, and the Democrats got away with it until President Clinton overdid it and blew their cover. Pity poor Bill Clinton. He is so much an emotive child of the sixties that he just can't help overdoing it. As president, he was so anxious to "feel our pain" that he forgot to be subtle. He was such a caricature of the "sixties man" that even the press finally understood the role he played of perpetrator as victim. He pushed the sophists too far. They finally had to either acknowledge his hamming or confess to being dupes themselves. After Clinton, everyone must admit that they understand the game, and, so, the jig is up. President Clinton's

mistake was that he got the cart before the horse and practiced the language of love as if it were an end unto itself. He
seemed on too many occasions to emote for effect without an
underlying political or policy objective. He made it too transparent. President Johnson had things in the right order. He
only used the language of love to disguise the politics of
greed, which was his true purpose.

In 1964 Lyndon Johnson understood the value of
dependency constituencies in politics. He used the illusion of
love for the elderly and "protected" them from Barry Goldwater to win the presidency. Johnson had not created that
constituency of dependency: seniors on Social Security.
Franklin Roosevelt had done that in the 1930s and perhaps
not even for political purposes. It is possible that Roosevelt
never understood the political value of dependency. He may
honestly have been trying to provide a way to improve the
lives of older Americans. Johnson saw that it was possible to
make the elderly feel threatened and insecure, profess his love
of them, ride to their rescue, and win an election. In that 1964
election year Johnson discovered the politics of fear, the politics of greed, the politics of class conflict, and the politics of
envy, and he could not wait to teach it all to his party.

Johnson quickly mastered the substance of the politics of
greed, but he never managed the style. He never could get
away from the good-old-boy, backroom-politician image of a
big beefy Texan. He could not get rid of the drawl. He had
little aesthetic appeal to the intellectual elite that was rapidly
coming to dominate his party. He was not suave and
debonair. He could conceive of the "Great Society" program
by program, but he could not carry it out on the public relations front. He was just not credible faking sincerity. What
was needed were some sixties men, not some "poor boy come
to greatness."

The Kennedy clan was the ticket. They and people like them were raised in privileged and enlightened circumstances. They were Ivy League educated and "sensitive." They were "empathic." They were "sincere." Also, they did not need the jobs. With their wealth and position they had plausible deniability if anyone accused them of being self-serving. They had the style to overcome high privilege and reach down to help the underprivileged and successfully feign altruism. They were clearly perceived to be in it only for the love. They moved comfortably from the society page to the front page. The eastern establishment easily identified with them. Guilty-feeling rich people found, in the Kennedy clan, a vicarious satisfaction of their need to be socially responsible. They were doing well for themselves while they were doing good for others. By throwing in glamorous lifestyles and movie stars, one had just the stuff to make a story called "Camelot."

The new Ivy League liberals were lowbrow enough to handle the substance of politics and highbrow enough to make even politics sufficiently ceremonial and socially acceptable. At last there was a respectful occupation for those not fit to be trusted with the family business. Let them tend to other people's business. That way, if they messed up, Mom, Dad, and the social set could still be proud of their service and their good intentions. Furthermore, those Ivy League crib courses and that sensitivity training could be put to use in pretty speeches, and the professors could be proud as well.

This was working out just fine. There was a renaissance in America. The intellectuals were hammering out the language of love and social responsibility, and the Democrats were writing it into law. All around us there were new rules of sensitivity, awareness, and relevance. The trick was simple. Search for victims and fix things for them. Divide the nation between the haves and the have-nots and help them to feel guilt or oppression, whichever was appropriate for their category. Then redistribute the wealth by taxation, spending, or mandate—whichever comes easiest. America had to get beyond "equality of opportunity" to equality of outcome.

This new great society would have a chicken in every pot and some pot for every chicken. It would be enlightened. People would have dialogues. They would love peace and make love, not war. Intellectuals would take their rightful place at the head of the class (conflict). Everyone else would be in their assigned place, dependent upon the government for food, shelter, employment, a living wage, education, health care, retirement, child care, public transportation, racial harmony, or all of the above. Each person would be the constituent of a government program. Each person could be scared into voting correctly by simply pointing out that the other candidate had a secret plan to abolish the program.

The Democrats became the party of love, always in touch with their feelings and never in touch with the facts, and they prospered. They were loved by the beautiful people and embraced by the Hollywood crowd and the intellectuals. The poor old Republicans were in touch with the facts and never comfortable with feelings—their own or anyone else's. Democrats had great style and charisma, and Republicans were boring. Democrats emoted over the poor and disadvantaged. Republicans tried to solve problems of "equimarginal conditions of allocative efficiency within multiple preference functions."

In fact, the Republicans were brighter and more sincere than the Democrats, but they lost elections because they had no style. Democrats exuded the image of enlightenment and sincerity, and they knew that in politics perception is reality. Republicans tried to create a real world of freedom and dignity born of personal responsibility. Democrats tried to create the perception of a world of freedom and dignity free from personal responsibility. As long as America went along with the essential ethos of the sixties and stayed in touch with its "inner child," the Democrats won elections.

President Clinton has, by his example, blown the whistle on the sixties. In his boyish boorishness America has seen what the sixties have come to, and America is embarrassed. In Clinton we saw the shallowness and superficiality of our own national sophomorishness, and we decided to grow up. All of President Clinton's self-indulgence, denial, and, victimology, along with the enabling behavior of those around him, debased the once-respected offices of this land. He felt our pain because he was our pain, and now we know it. We now want such antics out of our lives. That is why the Democrat party struggles. It must have a purpose other than itself, and it has lost any sense of what that might be. The politics of greed wrapped in the language of love, slick as it is, won't sell anymore. America has finally had enough of charisma, and now it wants character.

———————— ☙ ————————

There is nothing so arrogant as a self-righteous income redistributor

———————— ☙ ————————

K arl Marx expressed the issue of income redistribution as a choice between having people "give in accordance with their abilities and take in accordance with their contributions" and having them "give in accordance with their abilities and take in accordance with their needs." To some degree, nearly all political debate has that choice at its foundation. The question is, what is the fair way to divide up our output? If people are left to their own devices, they will take in accordance with their contributions and, by so doing, have every incentive to contribute their utmost. That proposition can be called *objective,* in that it describes what will happen voluntarily in a free society with no coercion. We will refer to it here as the *contribution ethic.*

The idea that people should give in accordance with their abilities and take in accordance with their needs is *normative.* We will refer to it here as the *need ethic.* It does not describe what people will do but, rather, what they should do. It requires third-party (government) enforcement to achieve both maximum contribution and the desired distribution. It also requires third-party judgment regarding which needs are legitimate, who has them, and in what amounts. The questions are who is to be that third party, and by what authority does he impose his will on others? Freedom lovers argue that this kind of authority and presumptions are not safely trusted to any one person, especially not to one with the folly and arrogance to think himself fit to exercise it.

Adherents of the need ethic, at their most idealistic, decry the use of force for its implementation. Their position is that if everyone was as good a person and as socially responsible as he should be, this ethic would prevail. To the extent people actually believe this, they are romantic egalitarians and more to be pitied than censured. Income redistributors believe it is necessary—in order to have a civil society as they define it—for them to compel others to behave *as if* they were altruistic, as they define it. Income redistributors must exercise control over others if they are to achieve the desired outcome. This is not an easy task, precisely because most people will put their immediate personal responsibilities ahead of abstract notions of social responsibility. They will resist.

Strangely enough, within today's "politically correct" rules of discourse, taking care of one's own business first is labeled *greedy*. Imagine that—the desire to work hard, obtain more, and keep it for yourself and your family is called greed. The desire to control the output of others, taking from those who earn more and giving to those who earn less, is called altruism. Much of the confusion might be cleared up by occasionally referring to dictionaries. Altruism is a willingness to give of your own wealth to someone else. In fact, adherents of the contribution ethic practice true altruism more than adherents of the need ethic.

Despite the fact that the contribution ethic is the most

natural and most influential in governing human intercourse, there is one venue in which the need ethic dominates. It is within our families. While we naturally insist on our fair share *as we earn it* with people outside the family, we also naturally accept far less within the family. This begins with parents, who contribute the most and often take the least. By their example, parents have the moral authority to impose the need ethic on others in the family. The children know it is right to share because they see Mom and Dad doing it first and most. The glue that makes this ethic stick is love.

Now here is the test: You love your family and would willingly give your life for them. Yet, how many times have you been upset, angry, irritated, or envious because someone in the family was getting more than their fair share? Come on now. Admit it. Your spouse spends too much on hobbies, entertainment, clothes, or the kids. The kids don't do a darn thing around the house and they get everything they want. Your brother-in-law is always mooching off you. You are not appreciated. Sis doesn't do anything to help out and she gets a new prom dress, while I work like a dog and can't have a new deer rifle. We are not buying any more Christmas presents for your folks until they remember little Angel's birthday. Not only must I work to support this family, but I also get stuck with all the housework. My folks gave us a European honeymoon, and yours gave us that cheap set of place mats. Sound familiar? We have all had those sentiments and with the people we know and love most, people for whom we would sacrifice everything. How, then, can we expect to live that same need ethic with strangers? If we are forced to do so, might we not build resentment where we would otherwise have positive feelings?

People are funny. Once they have earned their fair share and taken care of themselves and their family's needs, they share generously and voluntarily with others. They do this because it is in their hearts to do so. Americans are especially generous in this regard. People at all income levels do it. As they have more, they give more. But they cherish their right to do so voluntarily and at their own discretion.

Now comes the income redistributor. He knows better. He often gives little of his own and has disdain for private voluntary giving. Why? Because he does not control it. Things are not turning out to his liking so he seeks high office, authority, and power over others. The distribution of income must be made fair. He must first discredit all the reasons for income distribution as he finds it. To him, people don't have more because they earn more. Either they are lucky or they are crooks. There must be a distinction between "earned" and "unearned" income. And he will be the judge of that. He thinks it is not right for some to have so much and others so little. Never mind that those with much work harder, longer, or smarter. Never mind that those with much sacrifice immediate gratification in order to save and invest. Never mind that they are smart and creative. Never mind that they stayed in school, matriculated, and completed their theses. Never mind that they kept their noses clean and stayed out of trouble. Never mind that their parents worked hard to leave them the family business. Also, never mind all of the ways in which people with less might be responsible for their own plights. For income redistributors there is no excuse for some people having more than others.

The next thing the income redistributor does is to criticize the spending habits of the well-off. They indulge in "conspicuous consumption." They satisfy their material, nonessential, nonurgent needs. They are not socially responsible. Their houses and cars are too big and not environmentally friendly. They send their children to private schools and deny them a "multicultural experience." They don't pay their fair share of taxes. They give to private charities and undermine the role of government. Even when they are doing the same exact things with their income as the income redistributor, they are not doing it for the right, enlightened reasons.

Once the income redistributor has established, in his mind at least, that more than a fair share is going to the depraved and too little is going to the deprived, and once he has gotten himself into a position of power, he is ready to set things right. The first thing he needs is a "progressive" tax system. He must take a larger percentage of income from the well-off so they pay their "fair share." He must double- and triple-tax "unearned income" from property. He must impose "sin taxes" on consumption activities that meet with his disapproval. He must tax estates so undeserving children don't benefit from irresponsible parents. To the income redistributor, taxes are compensators and equalizers.

The next thing the income redistributor must do is to declare certain goods to be "rights." That way he can provide them for select constituencies he judges to have a high "relative social deservedness." He provides these products either through direct government expenditure often called "entitlements" or through mandates imposed on others. He can mandate a "living wage," an employee benefit package, or conditions for hiring and firing. He can use labor law or tort law and employ the legal profession in income redistribution. He can have publicly funded educational loan programs, health care, or housing. He is arrogant in his belief that he has morally and intellectually superior judgment and the moral authority to impose his will on others. His heart bleeds with other people's money and he stamps out the evils of "social Darwinism." His arrogance affords him a firm confidence that he knows the best and fairest outcomes. His self-righteousness is necessary to justify the means needed to fulfill his ends. While he insists that ends do not justify means for people minding their own business, it is imperative, because of his ethical, moral, and intellectual superiority, that he employ whatever means necessary to fulfill the ends he knows to be best and fairest.

My favorite example of the arrogant income redistributor is Charles Rangel from New York. Charlie is the ranking Democrat on the Ways and Means Committee. He describes himself as having "more self-esteem than what one needs to get by" and that is fair enough. He is a colorful character and a partisan of the first order. During a tax conference I argued that the best way to reduce taxes for people who actually pay taxes was to lower the 38 percent rate to 37 percent. I further argued that doing so would provide work incentives for the economy. My option would have reduced revenue (given a static analysis) by $12 billion over ten years. What Charlie wanted was to extend a tax rebate to all people who filed returns whether they paid taxes or not, thus giving a direct income transfer to non-taxpaying filers of up to $500. The cost of his option was $13 billion. In his exasperation with me for insisting that we ought to be cutting taxes for people who pay taxes rather than making tax transfers to people who did not pay taxes, Charlie said, "Armey, you are the worst income redistributor I have ever seen." Now you make sense out of that!

A little man can whip
a big man every time
if he's in the right and
keeps on a-comin'

I t is hard to say why this axiom is so much fun except that it is the motto of the Texas Rangers. Maybe that is all it needs to be. But, still, there must be a lesson in there somewhere. Certainly it is an admonition against discouragement. If you are in the right and you persist, you might prevail against the odds. Was that not true of David with Goliath? When Mother Teresa was asked why she continued to care for all the world's poor children, knowing she could not possibly succeed, she replied, "My job is not to succeed. My job is to try." Should we not continue to try even if we are not assured of success? How much would have been lost without people who tried and prevailed against all odds? Is there not something noble about believing you're right and trying the impossible?

On rare occasions we are privileged to watch someone with courage and convictions go through a period of anguish and emerge victorious and noble. To see someone "walk through the valley of the shadow of death" and "fear no evil because Thou art with me" is an inspiration. One such instance involved the confirmation of Justice Clarence Thomas to the Supreme Court. Justice Thomas is a good and decent man. He is a man of quiet dignity, respectful demeanor, and deep faith. His Senate confirmation should have been routine and pleasant. Unfortunately, it was not. Because Justice Thomas had been falsely accused, the committee was at an impasse.

The George Bush White House had subjected Clarence Thomas's nomination to the usual political "handling" in order to "work" the committee. In the face of false allegations, it was not looking good for Clarence's chances of confirmation. To his everlasting credit, Clarence dismissed his White House advisors and faced the committee on his own terms. Win or lose, he was going to deal with the issue as God intended: as his own man. In a hushed room, he faced the committee alone with his wife, Virginia, at his back. He gave a speech known to this day as the "High-tech Lynching Speech," words that should stir the hearts of brave men and women everywhere. The committee adjourned. During the ensuing few hours, before the committee reconvened for the confirmation vote, something extraordinary happened.

As a longtime friend of Clarence's, I had watched the whole episode and had been inspired by the speech. I remembered how I had once endured an incident of vicious false accusation, and I became concerned for Clarence. Clarence would have grave responsibilities on the Supreme Court, and I hoped to encourage him to put his hurt and anger aside in the face of those duties. I called Clarence to share my concern and offer encouragement. This call took place after the committee hearing and before the vote, during a period when Clarence's future hung in the balance and after a prolonged period of personal anguish for Clarence Thomas and his family.

As we spoke, Clarence said: "You know, Dick, the meanest thing about this whole episode is what they did to Anita Hill. They made a liar out of her, and she will have to live with that the rest of her life." Imagine that. His concern was for his accuser, not himself. He had compassion rather than anger and resentment. He urged me not to worry. His point was that it was in God's hands and God makes all things turn out for the good. I hung up the phone and told my wife not to worry. Clarence was going to be just fine, and he would make a fine Supreme Court justice.

As we know, the vote was taken. Clarence Thomas was confirmed, and despite the prejudice and hatred he faces each day, he is a fine Supreme Court justice with charity in his heart for his false accuser. Maybe someday Anita Hill and her cohorts will find redemption. Clarence already has his, and he prays for them to have theirs. Why did he win? Because he was in the right and he kept on a-comin'.

Armey's Axiom
Number 12

———————— ✻ ————————

No one spends someone else's money as wisely as he spends his own

———————— ✻ ————————

We are really the same, you know. I spend that money
like it is my money, and you spend that money like it is
my money.

—ARMEY TO LIBERAL BIG SPENDER

There are three identifiable groups of people who regularly spend other people's money: They are children, thieves, and politicians, and they all need adult supervision. The reason they need adult supervision is that they do not recognize costs, limits, and trade-offs like people who spend their own money. Because they don't earn the money, they don't know how hard it is to come by. They act as if money grows on trees. They tend to spend it all in one place without realizing that they won't be able to spend it elsewhere as well. We recognize these weaknesses in children and devote a lot of energy to teaching them how to spend money wisely. We do this because we know they are capable of learning and preparing for the day when they have only their own money to spend. We devote that time and effort to children because we love them and we respect their ability to learn. We don't do the same for thieves and politicians.

We are more likely to romanticize thieves and politicians. Poor babies, they are addicted to other people's money, and their intentions are so good. Robin Hood is the model. He robbed from the rich and gave to the poor. How noble is that? So did Jesse James, Bonnie Parker, Clyde Barrow, and Al Capone. So do Teddy Kennedy, Charlie Rangel, Jay Rockefeller, and Hillary Clinton. Jesse, Bonnie, Clyde, and Al defied the law to aggrandize themselves with other people's money. Teddy, Charlie, Jay, and Hillary make the law for the same purpose. Al Capone gave the poor a few dollars of other people's money to appear respectable in his greed for money. Charlie Rangel gives the poor a few dollars of other people's money to appear respectable in his greed for power. In neither case is the cost of earning the money given any respect. After all, it is other people's money: "Easy come, easy go." They may break a few eggs (or legs) to make egalitarian omelets, but it is such a noble undertaking. Why do we humor them? Why do we enable them? Because we neither respect their ability to learn nor love them. Unlike children, they are incapable of rehabilitation. We can't get rid of them, so we rationalize what they do. Isn't it a wonder what the heart can tell the mind?

When people spend their own money, they are careful to spend wisely. They shop. They compare. They ration. Everything they buy is considered against the next best alternative. They understand the limits of their finances and are careful not to waste. In so doing, they guide the nation to an efficient allocation of its resources and to that basket of goods that provides maximum happiness. They encourage neither surplus nor shortage of any product. It is, of course, inefficient to produce either a surplus or a shortage. In their effort to find the best deal and stretch their dollars, they fight inflation with every purchase. Such results do not follow when people spend other people's money foolishly. If money is no object, money is no object.

When Sir Francis Drake returned to English ports in the *Golden Hind* loaded with stolen Spanish gold he brought much joy to the queen and the royal court. He also brought much misery to the English people. Those large infusions of gold resulted in a redirection of productive effort to the luxuries of the court and away from the staples of the poor. There was a surplus of luxury goods and a shortage of staples. There was also, because of the sudden and uncontrolled infusion of gold, rampant inflation with its inevitable hardships, especially on the poor. Francis Drake robbed the Spanish, which was considered a good thing, and he was knighted. It turns out, however, that the Spanish were merely the middlemen in events that robbed the poor to give to the rich. Still, he got away with it and was loved by rich and poor Englishmen alike. As it is with money stolen and spent, so it is with money taxed and spent. In both cases the linkage between earning and spending the money is broken and the results are similar.

There is an old adage in economics: "If you want less of something, tax it. If you want more of something, subsidize it." Taxation results in shortages of those goods from which the taxes are generated. Subsidies result in surpluses of those goods. Hence government taxing and spending are inherently wasteful and inflationary. That does not make all government taxing and spending bad, but it should encourage us to keep them to a minimum.

In the aftermath of the so-called Great Society there were two sectors of American life that were afflicted by large and well-funded government spending programs. They were higher education and health care. In both cases there were huge increases in demand and rampant inflation. In both cases the American people had more but were less satisfied with what they had. Even after Ronald Reagan whipped general inflation, these two areas of American life still have costs spinning out of control. In both cases the increasing costs have made it almost impossible to obtain health care or higher education without a government subsidy.

That brings us to you and me. We, too, are part of this sordid story. How so, you ask? We spend only our own money. Well mostly, yes, but not altogether. Every American is, today, a party to some sort of third-party-payment system. It might be your automobile or homeowner's insurance. It might be your health insurance or, worse yet, your employer-provided health insurance. Well, you say, you pay the premiums. It is your money. True, but do you make a clear connection between the cost of your premiums and the cost of your claims? Most often that connection is vague and ill perceived, especially in the case of employer-provided insurance. When it comes time to acquire the service or make the claim, there is a great deal of unwise and excessive spending. Money is no object if you are covered. The doctor will order unnecessary procedures and you will take them if they are covered. As long as the fender dent is covered, let's include the rear panel. The body shop will include it in the estimate, and you will swear to the damage. There is no reason for us to deal with that kid's antisocial behavior. We are covered, so let's take him to a therapist. Responsible parental discipline would be cheaper and probably more effective. But, what the heck, we're covered.

Armey's Axiom
Number 13

————————— ☙ —————————

If it's about your power, you lose

————————— ☙ —————————

You shall have joy or you shall have power, said God;
you shall not have both.

—RALPH WALDO EMERSON

We all have many different kinds of relationships with other people. We can be peers, leaders, or followers. We relate in family, work, or social organization. In each case, we must give thought to our position in the relationship. Is it about status or stature? There is a difference. Status is about who I am, and stature is about what I do for others. If one pursues stature, one is likely to gain status. If one pursues status, one is likely to lose stature. The pursuit of status is about power and self, on a low road that leads only to heart-break and disappointment. The pursuit of stature is about service for others on a high road that leads to happiness and fulfillment.

Perhaps the most tragic consequence of modern-day American "sophistication" is the incessant lip service given to the pursuit of status. There is a popular mind-set that equates success with being powerful, feared, controlling, in charge, and guileful. Celebrated people, it is often argued, have such lofty goals that these goals may be pursued by any means possible. All too often even transparent pretension to service is admired, while real devotion to service is scoffed at as being naïve and simplistic. But, as Willie Nelson said, "It's not supposed to be that way."

The Lord God looked down on the children of Abraham wandering in the wilderness and encountering all manner of difficulty. He said, "I hope My children will know and obey My law so things will go well for them." He did not say, "They must obey Me and succumb to My power." His joy was not in demonstrating His power. His joy was in the hope for their happiness. At our best, we, too, hope to be a success in our own lives and a blessing in the lives of others. That can happen if we have a generous spirit and devote ourselves to serving others. That is our prayer for our children. That is what we pray for ourselves. Why then do we stray from our own hopes and prayers? It is because we allow ourselves to be seduced into a love of power. The siren song of power, if answered, will cause us only pain and hardship. Power is an illusion. It hurts both those who think they can exercise it and those who expect it to be exercised. Nevertheless, the higher the station, the greater the illusion of power. The illusion stems from confusion between status and stature. If one has stature, he is likely to have a moral authority by which he can persuade others. If he only has status, he is likely to suffer the illusion that he can compel others. And, he is likely to be frustrated.

President Harry S. Truman was given high marks for realism and humility when he said of himself as president of the United States: "The only power I have is the power to make a bunch of darn fools do what they ought to do anyway." In fact, he didn't even have that much power. What he had was the illusion of power because he was a man of some stature and he inhabited the Oval Office, which was a matter of some status.

He was able to use the status of his office and his personal stature to convince people to do many things, but he had no power to make them do anything. Even his much-celebrated affectation of humility was a delusion of power. Yet it stands as one of the more realistic observations in the folklore of American politics. Such is the strength of power's siren song. Still, Truman deserves a lot of credit for being minimally seduced by the trappings of his high office and the sycophancy it attracts. Too many people are not even that humble and perceptive. They are drawn to delusions of power. Otherwise well-intentioned people are often seduced to the delusion. They are more to be pitied than censured. Some people actually conspire to attain power. They are to be more censured than pitied.

The illusion of power is destructive because it sets up unrealistic expectations. The person who believes he has power is doomed to be frustrated when people won't do what he tries to make them do. Believing you are able to make people do things is the perfect prelude to overpromising. It also results in power struggles and stalemates. When I say "You will do this," and you say no, we both know there is more power in the no than there is in the "You will." The tragedy is that objectives that might have been attained through congeniality are instead lost through the assertion of power. The shame is that opportunity is lost to someone's vanity and ego. Rather than harmony, progress, and cooperation, the illusion of power begets disharmony, stalemate, and conflict. The self-possessed illusion of power is childish, and it inevitably results in childish, self-destructive behavior. Its frustration results in temper tantrums, depression, self-doubt, and any number of childish compensations like addiction and extramarital affairs. Indeed, lust for power can itself become an addiction, causing any number of perverse behaviors.

Not only does the illusion of power result in self-destruction, but it also results in disappointment for others. When one presumes power, others often believe it. When others believe you have the power to make things happen, they blame you when things don't turn out the way they expect. Their logic is simple. You have the power to make it happen. It does not happen. Therefore, you don't care, you don't try, you misrepresent your intention, or you misrepresent your power. Whatever the reason, they believe it is your fault that they don't get what they want. You are the one to blame, and blame you they do. You may not, in fact, be to blame for the failed outcome. Nevertheless, you are blamed because you either caused or allowed the illusion of your power. The power illusion for people in high office is so pervasive that it is a moral hazard that can be addressed only by the person holding that office. It is up to you to know your limitations and to be clear about them with others. If you do not, you are responsible for their unrealistic expectations and their disappointment.

If the search for status through the power model is doomed to failure, how can one fulfill a dream for success in one's own life and joy in the lives of others? The search for stature through the service model is the ticket. Get beyond yourself. Put others first. Don't worry about being someone. Worry about doing something. Don't commit your life to building your career. Commit your career to building lives. Do all things heartily as if unto the Lord. Whatever your position with its authority and responsibilities, promise only what you, yourself, can deliver, and commit only your best effort. If you divest yourself of the need to control and the illusion of power, you will be free to cooperate, persuade, and obtain the support you need to fulfill objectives. Do not hope to be feared and obeyed but rather to be appreciated and respected. If you commit to give until it hurts, you may find that it never does hurt. If you commit to take until it hurts, you will be in pain soon enough. If you give, you win. If you take, you lose. Finally, do not worry about who gets the credit. All glory is due the Lord. If our best athletes can know this on the playing field, why can't the best of us know this on the field of our dreams?

Armey's Axiom
Number 14

————— ⚜ —————

If you make a deal with the devil, you are the junior partner

————— ⚜ —————

This axiom has a nice ring to it, but it is not to be taken literally. People don't actually make deals with the devil. It just seems that way. But people do buy into "partnership" relationships that seem unholy. That is what extortion and blackmail are all about. If someone knows your dirty little secret and you agree to pay for his silence, you'll most likely pay forever. If an extortionist agrees not to harm you if you pay for protection from harm, you will most likely pay for a long time. In either case you cede some part of your autonomy to someone else, and they are likely, once they get their hooks into you, to want more. One thing will lead to another until they totally control you. Remember, if you marry for money, you'll earn every dime. The point is, be careful what you ask for. You might just get it.

It would be easy to make a substitution of only one word and have a more literal axiom. If you make a deal with the government, you are the junior partner. It is a common ploy of big government liberals to show up at your door and say,

"I'm from the government and I'm here to help you." When that happens, don't you believe it! They are really there to help themselves. They will propose a public/private partnership. That is the political equivalent of saying, "You and I could make beautiful music together," and it is a *proposition,* not a proposal. What it amounts to is that someone in the government has noticed that you are doing good things and getting credit for them, and that government person wants in on the action. Or it could mean that the government person wants to do something but cannot do it without your resources and cooperation. In either event, you can bet it is about them, not about you. So the big government liberal says, "Let's make a deal," and you fall for it. The deal is struck and you have a joint venture.

America's farmers fell for it. First, the government showed up to support their prices. Then they started to tell them what to grow. Then they started to tell them how much they could grow. Then they started to tell them who could grow what and how much on what land. It wasn't long before every farmer in America was a junior partner with the secretary of agriculture in managing his own land. It wasn't long until every banker checked the government's program qualifications instead of the farmer's agricultural qualifications before approving a loan. Then came the Environmental Protection Act, the Endangered Species Act, wetlands, soil conservation, the Farm Home Loan Guarantee, and foreclosure by the government. The junior partner is not bought out. He is driven out.

It's the same in the workplace. American business offers employee benefits to its workers. The government helps with tax breaks and technical advice. Soon the government begins to mandate. What had been mutually agreeable, voluntary, and beneficial employment terms soon becomes impositions not only on the employer but also on the employee. Recently, somebody in Washington decided all employees should have family and medical leave whether they wanted it or not, whether they needed it or not. Despite the fact that family and medical leave had never been sought in the history of collective bargaining agreements and despite the fact that mandating the benefit meant other benefits would be dropped in many cases, the government forced the benefit on employers and employees alike. Family and medical leave was not of sufficient value to be sought in private transactions. But someone in the government thought people *should* want it so they mandated a benefit that was not needed and would be little used by the vast majority of workers. The junior partner must take what he gets and like it. Likewise as an employer, you get a tax break if you provide health insurance. That is a good thing to do. The government wants to partner with you in doing it. Soon the government mandates what coverage the insurance package must include, for whom, and for how long. The result is that employers are forced to provide, and employees are forced to accept, insurance coverage that goes far beyond what either would voluntarily buy. Still, if we look at it from the viewpoint of big government, the junior partner can't be trusted to make such important decisions. And so it goes.

————————— ⚜ —————————

If you want the divorce, you give up the house

————————— ⚜ —————————

This axiom is not very attractive, and it should not be taken too literally. It is not just about the heartbreaking subject of divorce, but, in a larger sense, about how to end an unhappy relationship. Life is about relationships, contracts, commitments, entanglements, and associations. They often do not turn out the way we expect them to, and we often want to end them. But relationships and other commitments do not just happen. They are formed out of mutual expectations and they imply give and take. When one party seeks to terminate the relationship, it is unrealistic to assume that the other party will readily forsake the benefits that brought the two people together in the first place. That is where the expression "You owe me" comes in. It is also unreasonable to expect the other party to continue to extend the benefits of the relationship while letting the disappointed one off the hook and out of the deal.

Most associations are formed voluntarily out of shared expectations that "we will make beautiful music together."

91

Voluntary associations are often romanticized at their inception, which results in unrealistic expectations and subsequent disappointments. We should take a partner "warts and all" if we expect the partnership to last. Without a rigorous, disciplined realism few things are what they seem. Most things turn out to be bitter disappointments or pleasant surprises. Pleasant surprises are hard to come by in associations formed of blind love, and few things put us in touch with our "inner child" more quickly than when we must deal with disappointment.

Sometimes associations are not voluntary. They involve shotgun weddings, marriages of convenience, or politicians who have become strange bedfellows. In these instances expectations and disappointments are not the problem. The likelihood for pleasant surprises is actually greater because no generosity is expected. Nevertheless, the chances for a failed relationship are great because there are usually conflicting agendas. Still, in the absence of the expectation that we will get everything we want, it is possible to make a decent compromise and achieve the objectives that motivated the association. The person who wants the deal the most will be the person who must give the most. One can either be the pursuer or the pursued. It is always best to be the pursued. That's why playing hard-to-get is good strategy in a courtship. That's why being indifferent to the outcome or, better yet, trusting it to the Lord is powerful. It is better to negotiate from indifference than from anxiety.

How does one terminate an association? There are many ways. Some are honorable and realistic. Others are not. For example, it is best if both parties agree that the relationship isn't working, so both agree to settle up and end it. That rarely happens. More often one party wants the settlement, and the other does not. It is reasonable to declare, "I don't want any more cheese, I just want out of the trap," if you mean it. But don't expect to get out of the trap and take the cheese with you. The other party has a right to expect you to give it up if you want out. If you come to the settlement table wanting something, you better be prepared to pay for it. Do not believe you can make the other party settle on your terms. There is great power in the word no and no power in the phrase "You must."

The recent sensational defection from the Republican party by Senator Jim Jeffords is a good example of how not to end a relationship. Senator Jeffords was always too liberal to be a comfortable fit with the Republicans, but he was never alone in that department. His liberal ways were a problem for years, but they were never a world-class issue until 2001, when George W. Bush took office along with a slim Republican majority in the House and a fifty/fifty split in the Senate, which became a Republican majority with the vote of Vice President Cheney, president of the Senate. Senator Jeffords brought the issue of his liberalism to a head when he voted against the president's first budget and set off a firestorm of denunciations.

Given that Senator Jeffords's vote was consistent with his long legislative record and that the fifty/fifty Senate had a Republican majority only by counting the vice president, Republicans should have shown more forbearance than they did. Majority Leader Trent Lott made a great deal of noise about how Jeffords needed to be disciplined and the many ways he might do that. When President Bush, who made it a point to hug liberal Democrats in public, held a White House reception for the National Teacher of the Year from Vermont, he pointedly did not invite her Republican senator and the chairman of the Senate Education Committee, Senator Jeffords, to the event. That omission was a breach in protocol that should not have been visited on any senator for any reason. All this made it almost imperative for the senator to quit the Republican party. I don't know how he could have done otherwise. By their actions and rhetoric Majority Leader Lott, President Bush, and other Republicans made it clear that they wanted Senator Jeffords to leave the party. He came to that conclusion and he left the GOP.

Senator Jeffords catapulted from head of an anonymous caucus to greater celebrity than at any time in his long congressional career. He became the man who changed history. What he changed was the fifty/fifty Republican majority in the Senate to a fifty/forty-nine Democrat majority. Majority Leader Lott won the right to be minority leader, and the president won the right to deal, instead, with Democrat Majority Leader Tom Daschle. Vice President Cheney won a diminished role in the Senate. The Republicans wanted the divorce, and while they didn't give up the House, they gave up the Senate.

———————— 🌿 ————————

Politics sooner or later makes a fool out of everyone

———————— 🌿 ————————

I came to Washington to change the world. Now I just
want to get out with a little dignity.

—CONGRESSMAN HENRY HYDE

W hen people seek elective office, they generally do
so with the highest ideals. They have principles,
and they intend to keep them without compromise. For the
most part they do just that. Whether liberal, conservative, or
moderate, most people in high office retain their essential values and represent them well. But everyone discovers sooner or
later that politics requires compromise. This begins with the
conflict between whether a representative is supposed to represent the ideals on which he ran for office or the interests of
his constituency. Politicians must get elected and reelected if
they are to hold office and represent their ideals and values.
They also must be accountable and responsive to important
constituencies. The question is on behalf of which constituencies will the officeholder choose to compromise himself.

Most officeholders will compromise their own beliefs in
deference to voters' concerns over social or economic policy.
Some will compromise in the interests of their financial contributors. Some will compromise out of a desire to be loved

by the "beautiful people." The first of these is understandable and necessary. The second two are optional and undignified. It is one thing to put the interest of your constituents over your own and quite another to put your personal political interests over those of your constituents. Coping with all these pressures requires maturity on the part of the office-holder. Before seeking office, you must know who you are and what you stand for. You must also be candid about that with those whose votes you are seeking. People will always respect a person who does in office what he said he would do while he was seeking office. On the other hand, if you don't know who you are before seeking or taking office, someone is going to own you before very long.

The need to "bring home the bacon" by bringing government spending to your district or state is the most commonplace dilemma officeholders face. It is an unsavory business for fiscal conservatives. Too many people seeking office say they will work to bring benefits to their constituents because they think they must in order to be elected. In doing so, they let themselves in for an unnecessary bother. If that is not going to be your tendency while in office, don't advertise a willingness to do it while seeking office. How can you later say, "I never promised you a rose garden" if that is, in fact, what you did promise? You are responsible for the expectations you create, and you will be held to them. So if you don't want to do "pork," don't say you will do it. Nevertheless, it will be expected of you, and if it is of significant interest to your constituency, you will do it. That may be peanut subsidies in Georgia, tobacco subsidies in North Carolina, ethanol in Iowa, shipyards in Philadelphia, or heating oil subsidies in New York City.

In Texas recently it was the superconducting supercollider. This was a huge public works project promising many permanent jobs and much economic benefit from esoteric research in the physics of superconductivity, whatever that is. At any rate it was a large amount of money in the federal budget. I, as a fiscal conservative, decided to see if it met my high standards for spending money. I thought it should have a high enough potential for national benefit to justify the expense. I questioned the science community. What I found was that biologists, chemists, most engineers, and most physicists discounted the science. Only those physicists and engineers who did that kind of research embraced the science. I saw that the science community was perfectly capable of having its conclusions shaped by where they thought federal research money might be spent. It is not only lawyers who chase ambulances.

I discovered two other things while researching the superconducting supercollider. First, when it was first proposed, there was a site selection competition between Texas, Illinois, and California. Prior to the selection of Texas as the site, all three state delegations in Congress argued in support of the project. After the selection, only the Texas delegation argued for its passage. Second, once Texas was selected, the entire state wanted it. It was soon clear that any Texan who voted against the superconducting supercollider just because he had a doubt about its long-term economic and scientific benefits was not going to very popular in the Lone Star State. What did I do?

I knew I did not understand superconductivity or its long-term scientific value. I also knew that my constituents expected me to vote for it and that they were going to be pretty upset if I voted no. I feared that voting yes might be a crazy thing to do. But I remembered an old saying "I might be crazy but I am not stupid." I also remembered that old saying "If you're going to go ugly anyway, go ugly early." When the vote was called, I stepped right up and cast one of the first yes votes. With a sigh of resignation I took my turn at letting politics make a fool out of me. To this day I feel foolish about that vote. The superconducting supercollider is no more. It fell victim to the budget cutters. The nation doesn't seem to miss it. But my constituents remember I tried. I console myself by thinking about what might have been. The superconducting supercollider might have been a musically talented middle linebacker for the Dallas Cowboys. It might, then, have made more sense.

It is one thing to vote against your better judgment because your constituents expect you to. It is quite another to do so because your contributors expect it of you. An elected representative is chosen by his constituents. He chooses his campaign contributors. Constituents and their interests go with the territory. Special interest contributors are optional and can be found anywhere. While it is fairly easy to understand a person voting against his values in the interest of his constituents, it is hard to understand doing so for a special interest contributor. That is not loyalty. That is not service. That is not representation. That is prostitution. It is never acceptable to cast a vote for the purpose of protecting your contributor file. The officeholder who does this becomes something worse than a fool. He has put a price on his integrity. Once the world knows what he is, it needs only to haggle over the price.

There is something lower than selling your vote for money. That is selling your vote for love, or something like it. That is a common dilemma for conservatives. They vote for things like the National Endowment for the Arts or Humanities because they want to be appreciated on the cocktail circuit. They vote for direct student loans because they want to be welcomed by college faculty. They make "politically cor-rect" votes to please the Hollywood crowd. They seek favor-able editorials. They try to appease the left. It is a demeaning and undignified exercise in "looking for love in all the wrong places." The first rule of conservatism is to accept the fact that if you are true to yourself, Susan Sarandon will never hug you in public. If a person casts his vote in the pursuit of love or money, it isn't politics that makes a fool out of him. He makes a fool out of himself.

Political ambition is a great compromiser

It is one thing, once you are in office, to put your prefer-ences aside and vote with those of your constituents. After all, you work for them and you have an obligation to represent them. Because they elected you, they have a right to be represented by you. It is quite another thing to vote contrary to your own inclinations and those of your constituents to satisfy the wishes of a future constituency of some desired future office. Yet this is done all the time, and it bothers me. It goes against being one's own man. It also demonstrates that a man cannot serve two masters—in this case, one's current constituents and one's desired future constituents. It is, in short, a bad business. The principal cause of this aberration is political ambition. The desire for higher office can make a darn fool out of anyone. Knowing this, I am proud to say I never encumbered myself with political ambition. I believe it has saved me a lot of embarrassment.

I first recognized this aberrant behavior in a U.S. House member who was running for the U.S. Senate. The member voted with the Rio Grande Valley against the interests of his current panhandle constituents on the theory that he would need votes from the valley for his Senate race. He lost. I later saw a Ph.D. economist, who was a senator from Texas, and an East Coast publisher of a major business journal both pledge their support of ethanol to Iowa corn farmers in order to stay in the primary campaign for president. They both lost.

Political ambition does not manifest itself only in the quest to leave one office for another. It can also be seen in the effort to rise to a leadership office within a body. The case of U.S. congressman Jim Wright comes to mind. Jim Wright was a Texas Democrat at a time when Texas Democrats were often more conservative than many northern Republicans. Wright wanted to be the Speaker of the House of Representatives. In his heart of hearts Jim Wright was a conservative Texas Democrat. Yet for Wright to be Speaker he had to make peace with the liberal majority of Democrat House members. He did this by acting as if he were one of them. That left the folks in Fort Worth disappointed that he had become a liberal. They accepted his departure from their values because as Speaker, he did a better job of bringing home the bacon. Still every form of refuge has its price. Years after his retirement, Wright lamented that the liberals had "ruined his life." Actually, insofar as his life was ruined, it was his own political ambition that was the cause, not the liberal Democrats in the House.

I, too, went through the experience of rising in House leadership. My experience was different from Wright's because I defeated the Republican establishment rather than conforming to it. My adventure in House leadership came out of my frustrations with Dick Darman during the first Bush presidency. Early in 1989 I discovered an effort by Leon Panetta, chairman of the House Budget Committee, and Dick Darman, President Bush's budget director, to convince

President Bush to raise taxes in 1990. I knew that America would not accept the betrayal of Vice President Bush's famous "Read my lips" campaign promise in spite of Darman's ill-conceived advice to the contrary. I began sounding the alarm against this risky tax scheme in January of 1989. Darman successfully discounted my efforts until a moment of truth when, out of desperation, I passed the "Armey resolution" against tax increases in the House Republican Conference in June of 1990. That event was too public and I regretted it, but I had been shut out of President Bush's White House and denied the opportunity to persuade the president more privately. I did, however, want to spare my House colleagues from embarrassment and future political losses. I was not altogether successful in that effort. I can cite three House members who lost their Senate bids and six more who were not reelected to the House because they voted in favor of the 1990 Bush tax increase. Not a single Republican lost for voting no.

Needless to say, I did not stop the tax increase, and Republicans paid through the nose in the 1990 and 1992 elections. Despite the fact that I had no personal political ambition, I decided in the aftermath of that debacle to run for leadership. It was only because I refused to be locked out of the White House in the future that I decided to run. I ran for Republican Conference chairman against the opposition of the White House and the entire House leadership. When I won, the local press asked my son, Scott, if that meant that his dad had joined the establishment. I am so proud that he replied, "No! That means my dad beat the establishment." Lucky me. My first meeting at the White House after joining the House leadership was with President Clinton, who thought it was a fine idea for George Bush to have raised taxes in 1990. Later we won the majority, and I became majority leader, a position I held until I retired from Congress.

The big difference between former Speaker Jim Wright and myself was that the majority of my majority was conservative like myself and the majority of his majority was liberal while he was conservative. The moral of the story is that if you are a square peg trying to fit into a round hole, you will have to reshape yourself. Jim did that. I was lucky in that I never had to meet that test. I like to believe that I would never want any office enough to redefine myself in order to get it. Still one should have caution about taking pride in one's own character, especially in comparison to others, when one has never been required to meet the same test.

———— ⚜ ————

A man will fight like a cornered rat if his chicken manure is at stake

———— ⚜ ————

S enator Bill Roth from Delaware, chairman of the powerful Senate Finance Committee, inspired this axiom in
the summer of 2000. Senator Roth, famous for Roth IRAs,
was a dedicated writer of tax law to benefit his constituency.
This drove Bill Archer, the powerful chairman of the House
Ways and Means Committee, to distraction. Bill Archer was a
dedicated generic tax writer who openly disdained "rifle
shots" for parochial interests. Bill Archer also considered it
self-serving and undignified to name legislation after oneself.
It was his view that the law was the law of the land, not of the
person privileged to write it. Bill Archer was the most professional person I ever worked with in Congress. For Bill, it
was always about service to the nation. It was never about
himself. Oh, how I admired that and tried to emulate him.

Although I was never privileged to serve on the Ways
and Means Committee, I am an economist by training, and
for that reason I was always the House Republican leadership
representative to the tax-writing process. Both Speakers

Newt Gingrich and Dennis Hastert appointed me to the tax-writing conference committees charged with working out differences between the House and the Senate. Many times Archer and I were the only House Republican conferees. Therefore, I was always able to see firsthand what the senators brought to the table.

In the year 2000, a presidential election year in which Bill Roth was up for reelection against the very popular governor Tom Carper, we passed through the House and to the Senate a substantial increase in Roth IRAs. The iron was hot. The House vote count was a very bipartisan 400+, and the president would have had to sign it into law if the Senate moved it fast. But, alas, Bill Roth refused to move it. He chose instead to wait for a larger tax bill at the end of the year. This bewildered us, since it was Roth's big legacy and he was in a tight election. This seemed like madness to Archer and me, but that madness had a method to it and we soon enough discovered it when we finally went to conference with the Senate on the larger tax bill.

No sooner had the conference opened than we were stunned by Roth's demand for the most insane tax provision since ethanol. Roth had a special tax sop that involved making methane out of chicken manure. We, of course, would have thought it a joke from anyone but Senator Roth, but we could see the seriousness and resolve in his face. Even though our initial reaction was that this was chicken manure, we soon realized that we were going to have to find a way to make chicken salad out of chicken manure. We urged Roth not to count his chickens before they were hatched, but he was determined. We thought that if we were both very angry he might chicken out, but he persevered. When we told him that the nation's voters would rise up in revolt and throw us all out of office, he accused us of being Chicken Little. We told him that we would have egg on our face. He reminded us that you have to break a few eggs in order to make an omelet. We said it would cost too much. He said it was only chicken feed. We scratched and pecked at him for weeks, but he rose every morning at dawn and crowed about the new day this would bring to America. Archer wanted to wring his neck, and I wanted to roast him. He remained undeterred. We walked away from the table, but he roosted on it for two more weeks. Time was running out, and we were in the soup. Still the fox remained vigilant as he guarded the henhouse.

I finally relented and went along with Senator Roth. I did this, of course, only for honorable reasons: the good of the order and all that. I did it in the interest of the larger tax bill. I did it because leaders must lead. I deserved a lot of credit for my leadership. Bill Archer was sooo understanding. He loved me, you know. He treated me to every chicken expression he knew, with me as the object of his affection. He reminded me of my infidelities. He cursed the day I was born. He said insincere things about my mother. If I had had a dog, he would have kicked him. He said my wife was a darn fool for marrying me. He told me not to darken his door again or he would shoot me. I began to worry about our friendship. Still, I knew it would get better, if only because it could not get worse. We moved the bill from Congress to the White House and breathlessly awaited presidential validation. Roth prepared his press releases and fund-raising letters to the nation's chicken farmers. Archer was sooo kind. He told me that I could go to the signing ceremony if there was one.

The president vetoed the tax bill. Bill Roth lost his election. Bill Archer retired. Sometime later, while in my local credit union, I observed a large bulletin board listing Roth IRAs. I thought, what a nice legacy for Bill. It was too bad he hadn't realized what a big deal it was.

I still see Bill Archer every now and then, and we laugh over the big chicken manure caper. Still, things can never be the same, given what he had said about my mother and all. But here is the irony. Bill Roth was defeated. Bill Archer and I are both retired. But the chicken manure lives on. Someone, maybe Senator Tom Carper, will someday reintroduce the chicken manure tax credit in the name of an energy crisis, and it will probably be enacted.

As bizarre as it seems, it is possible to understand and even accept members of Congress trying to enact chicken manure tax credits for their constituents' business interests. What is neither understandable nor acceptable is a member who legislates his own heartbreak. A senator whose daughter had an allergy to peanuts astounded me when he put a rider on a transportation-spending bill to prohibit airlines from serving peanuts. How nutty is that? Apparently not too nutty, since our House chairman went along with it because his daughter also had allergies. Then there was the senator whose daughter suffered from mental illness, and he added tens of billions of entitlement spending to the budget to cover such cases. Again members of both houses went along with it because of his family experience. Talk about bleeding your heart with other people's money! In these cases personal testimonies abound and empathy floods the floor for our stricken colleagues and their families. As long as the nation can afford it, congressmen will take care of their families and their afflictions.

Now don't get me wrong. Many of those maladies about which legislators emote when they or their families are affected deserve the attention of the federal government. However, they should be weighed objectively against one another with regard to their overall benefit to the American people and the extent to which the government can effectively pursue policies with a good chance of alleviating them in the public interest. One should not be bumped ahead in the legislative queue simply because someone in a privileged position experienced a particular affliction in his own life. My point is that people elected to high office have no right to legislate their own heartaches. It is self-serving and ought to be beneath the dignity of their office. Yet they do it, and when they do it, they fight like cornered rats. For some people there are no words so compelling as the words "You owe it to yourself."

It's a wonder how much
will get done when
people are concerned with
who gets the credit

R onald Reagan kept a little sign on his desk that read: "It's a wonder how much can get done when no one is concerned with who gets the credit." That is, indeed, a laudable sentiment, and one that is often cited and to which much lip service is given. But, as Sportin' Life said, "It ain't necessarily so." It is natural for people to want credit for their good works. In fact, it is not uncommon for people to want credit for the good works of others. It is unusual for anyone to be indifferent about getting the credit. Indeed, I can think of few instances where that was the case. What is amusing is the length to which people will go both to get credit and to milk the credit they can get. For example, the hallmark of the first two years of the Reagan administration was the Gramm-Latta budget put together in the House of Representatives by then Democrat Phil Gramm of Texas and Republican Del Latta of Ohio. The loud and raucous quarrel between these two men over whether it was to be Latta-Gramm or Gramm-Latta is legendary. Somehow it turned out to be Gramm-

Latta. It was passed, and it set the stage for Reagan's economic policy. It also got Phil Gramm removed from the Budget Committee by the Democrats. This, in turn, caused him to resign from Congress, change parties, and be reelected as a Republican. Gramm, it turns out, is as mean as a Democrat and as smart as a Republican. He went on to become an outstanding Republican senator from Texas. It is clear that much good came from that case precisely because someone cared about who got the credit.

My first realization that getting the credit is important came in my second term in Congress. During the years 1987 and 1988, I did what I now realize was a truly remarkable piece of legislating. As a second-term member of Congress, I made what may have been the largest single change in national defense policy during the time I was in Congress. That was the Base Realignment and Closure Act (BRAC). The act set aside a law that had prevented any base closures for over ten years. I understood early that I could pass the BRAC only with a lot of outside help, because the Washington establishment was organized against it. I turned to the editorial pages, beginning with an op-ed piece, coauthored by Barry Goldwater, in the *New York Times.* I then received a supportive editorial from the *Times* itself and painstakingly shopped them around the country until I had an editorial drumbeat to "pass the Armey base-closing bill." I knew it was important to identify the bill with myself in order to beat down efforts to defeat BRAC by supplanting it with something that looked like it but would not do the job.

Congressmen are peculiar people. They read the editorial pages before they read the sports pages. They understand that even if editorials are not often read, they reflect the views of the hometown paper. There is an old adage in politics: "Never upset anyone who buys their ink by the barrel." Being aware of this, every time I found someone whose vote I needed, I got a supportive editorial in his hometown newspaper. It actually got to the point where people wanted to vote for what Armey wanted on base closing. This desire was not born out of respect or admiration for Dick Armey but out of a fear of getting an uncomplimentary editorial back home.

I ginned up a lot of publicity for "the Armey base-closing bill." I was getting a lot of attention, which was noticed by my colleagues. One day while returning from Dallas to Washington I encountered a colleague on the plane. His exact words were: "You know, Dick, the reason you are getting all this attention for base closing is you are acting as if you really want to shut down military bases." That really stunned me. It never occurred to me that someone might have considered my efforts to be less than genuine. It never occurred to me that someone might think I was doing something only for the attention. It did dawn on me that others might trifle in such a way. Can you imagine not wanting to do something but wanting the attention instead? A seat in Congress is a terrible thing to waste on one's ego or vanity. Nevertheless, "I meant what I said and I said what I meant. An elephant's faithful one hundred percent." Base closing was passed into law in 1988.

When the base-closing bill finally passed Congress to be sent to the White House for President Reagan's signature, I stood on the floor after the vote and enjoyed the moment. A dear friend, Joe Moakley from Massachusetts, approached me. Joe was the second-ranking Democrat on the powerful Rules Committee, who, despite his opposition to the bill, had helped me many times along the way. He had been kind and encouraging when there was no good reason to be so. Joe said something to me at that moment that was a revelation. His exact words were: "You know, Armey, you are a darn fool to finish that in two years. You could have milked that for years to come." I mean no criticism of Joe, because I remember him with great fondness, but did his words suggest that people would actually do that? Would people actually delay something they thought good for the nation and long overdue just to get more years of credit for it? A hard-fought legislative victory of a lifetime is a terrible thing to waste on a man's ego or vanity.

What did I get out of base closing? I got a trip to the Oval Office with my wife to watch President Reagan sign the bill. I got a signed copy of the bill and President Ronald Reagan's pen. To this day I am known for base closing. I also got my picture hung on the dartboard of a bar just outside a base that was closed. Once again something had gotten done precisely because someone cared who would get the credit for it. Had it not been for the national editorial insistence on passing the Armey base-closing bill, it would not have been passed.

During my first term in Congress, East German border guards shot and killed a young Major Nicholson. We were outraged. I put together a resolution to condemn the atrocity. Time was of the essence. We needed that resolution on the floor as soon as possible. The Committee on Rules referred the resolution to the Foreign Affairs Committee, for which Gerald Solomon from New York was the ranking Republican on the minority side. My young staff assistant Peter Davidson went to the minority staff on the committee and asked for their help. They allowed as how the resolution could be moved quickly with one little change. Simply remove my name as the author and replace it with Gerald Solomon's. The deed was done, and the resolution passed unanimously. Some young committee staff member, I'm sure, received a lot of credit for that resolution from his boss. Ten years later, while on the floor with Gerald Solomon, we passed a resolution commemorating the ten-year anniversary of Major Nicholson's death. Solomon turned to me and reminded me that he had passed a resolution condemning the East Germans at the time. It was only at that moment that I realized it wasn't Gerry who had wanted the credit, but his staff. Given that the committee staff might not have been willing to do the work had I been unwilling to give it up, I conclude that once again something had gotten done precisely because someone wanted the credit.

In 1995 and 1996 the new Republican majority in the United States House of Representatives reformed welfare for the first time in its history. President Clinton vetoed the reform two times, condemning it as the personification of Republican heartlessness. He finally signed it, over the protest of Vice President Al Gore, just before the elections of 1996. Welfare reform turned out to be a great success. Millions of people left welfare for work. Teenage pregnancy decreased for the first time in a generation. The public was pleased, and the pundits praised the effort. President Clinton left office celebrating welfare reform as one of his "best accomplishments" even while he continued to condemn the Republicans. Even Vice President Al Gore, who had fought it up to the moment it was signed into law, celebrated it as one of his best ideas when running for president in 2000. There you have it. A good idea has a thousand parents, while a bad idea is an orphan. People, it turns out, will even take credit for the good things they never did and even resisted. Nothing is so attractive as an idea that turns out well.

Insecurity is an audacity in light of the Lord's promise: "I will never leave you nor forsake you"

Insecurity is, perhaps, the most harmful of emotions. There are others that, on the surface, are meaner, such as greed, envy, malevolence, or anger, but they almost always elicit feelings of guilt and are, therefore, suppressed. Insecurity is, on the other hand, more insidious because the wrong of it is less easily perceived. Insecurity is an anxiety that derives from a fear of being misunderstood or mistreated. If our insecurities are not understood and controlled, they can lead to destructive behavior. As Shakespeare says: "Our fears do make us traitors."

I have thought long and hard on this, and it is true for me. It might also be true for you. Nearly every hurtful or mean thing I ever did in my life was done while I was feeling insecure. It stems from that impulse to do unto others before they can do unto you. While we strike out from our insecurity, it almost always comes across to others as arrogance. And so we are misunderstood, not because others don't understand us, but because we don't understand ourselves. When others react in the most predictable way to our folly, we become even more convinced that our worst fears are real and that we are misunderstood. So we repeat the process over and over, always expecting a different result until something really bad happens.

Assuming that you are, in your heart of hearts, truly a good person who does not intend harm to others, what can you do about these insecurities? The first is to be introspective. An unexamined life isn't worth living. There are mean, greedy, envious, malevolent, and angry people out there. If they really are out to get you, you are not paranoid. Such people are usually quite skillful and cannot be effectively confronted. They plan and scheme and enlist the help of others. They are ruthless and difficult to confront. They are masters of the scenario where they, as perpetrators, are able to convince others that they are victims. These are the people who create office politics, and they are found in every walk of life. They are almost impossible to manage. What to do?

First, understand that if you can perceive them for what they are, others can, too. If your boss had the good sense to see you were the man for the job, why would you doubt that he understands your tormentor any less? If he has connived against you, he will have done so against others. Remember that "time wounds all heels." You can afford to ignore him because he doesn't have credibility. Eventually you will be his boss, and he will be the first to curry your favor. That is the time to give favor to someone more deserving. Don't think you can rehabilitate him. If his parents failed to raise him properly, why should you take him to raise? Just move on. He will be a distant memory soon enough because he isn't going anywhere.

Second, resist the temptation to "set the record straight." That just gets you into a spraying contest with a skunk, and unless you can shut him down, he'll have it all over you. Remember, people like that know it is better to be persecuted than ignored. So, ignore them. Also, remember, when you tell people your troubles, 90 percent of them don't care and the other 10 percent are glad you have them. Furthermore, as in the motto of Dick's Last Resort, "You can't shoot a man born to be hanged" and "They can't hurt a man that doesn't give a hoot." If you hit a skunk in the road, drive on. Don't go back to check on it. It is not going anywhere. Unless you let your anxieties betray you, you have nothing to fear from these little people. In office politics as in politics, your audience is a world of third parties and you must rely on their good sense. Fortunately, that is usually good ground on which to stand.

Now for the more difficult case, when you are the perpetrator rather than the victim. What do you do when you have examined your life and you find that you are your own worst enemy? You say that nobody understands you. You are not appreciated. They are out to get you. You aren't getting paid what you are worth. Your boss is an idiot, and by rights, you should be his boss. It sounds like you are a moneymaker. You ought to buy yourself for what you're worth and sell yourself for what you think you're worth. Nevertheless, to be honest, it is your bad attitude born out of your insecurities that gets you in trouble. How can you fix that?

If insecurity is bedeviling you, and you do not think you can repair your life as it is, you can trade your life in for a new one. You can be born again. That is what I did. For me, the free gift of salvation paid for, on the cross, by my Lord Jesus Christ fixed my problem with insecurity. If He be for you, who can be against you? If the blood of the Lamb covers you, what harm can come to you? I have no doubt that Holy Scripture is the written word of God. In it, He gives us Ten Commandments, a whole lot of good suggestions, and even more promises. The commandments are to be obeyed, and that should not be difficult for decent people. The suggestions should be taken. So things will go well for you. The promises should be cherished. When God says: "I know the plans I have for you, plans to prosper you not to harm you," how can you be insecure? When God says: "I will never leave you nor forsake you," how can you be insecure? When the Lord Jesus is your advocate before God His Father, He will not make your case from the pages of newspapers or office memos. He will not consult your raw FBI file. No, He will make your case from what is in your heart. He is that advocate you wanted all those times you felt insecure. Now that I know, I believe God is in His Heaven. He has prepared a place for me. He protects me. In light of that, I now know that insecurity is the audacity of little faith. I have no doubt that I am a person of worth. God sent His only Son to die a horrible death on the cross for my sake. If God in His Heaven values me that much, how dare I be insecure?

I had the opportunity to share this with Newt Gingrich once. During all of 1998 I was under constant attack from people both inside and outside of the House of Representatives. It seemed as though the false accusations and constant intrigue would never end. It was an unrelenting assault, and it seemed to come from all directions. One day Newt and I had breakfast in downtown Washington. While I was eating my breakfast, Newt exclaimed: "How can you do that"? I responded: "Do what?" "Just sit there calmly eating your eggs when the whole town is out to get you. People are accusing you of everything under the sun and plotting to drive you out of office. I could never sit there that calmly if they were after me that way." I explained to Newt that this was not the first time I had suffered such an attack. From 1977 to 1983 I had been attacked in much the same way with similar falsehoods at the university. At that time I was so insecure and felt so alone and became so obsessive and crazy that Susan almost left me. I almost lost the one person on this earth that I loved the most over worry about people who didn't like me and for whom I had no respect. The problem was that at that time, I was going it alone. This time I am going through it with Jesus. I have no fear and no insecurity because the blood of the Lamb covers me. Newt thought about it, but said nothing. I wish he had asked for more information.

———————— ⚘ ————————

Liberals love feelings too much, conservatives love facts too much

———————— ⚘ ————————

I have often wondered why some people are liberal and others are conservative. What is it that attracts people to one path or the other? The question is not about the difference between a liberal and a conservative. The question is why we choose to be one or the other. Thomas Sowell, in his book *A Conflict of Visions,* gives a good explanation of the philosophical and political heritage of the two options. The intellectual underpinnings are clearly understood. But let's face it. Few people think as deeply as Thomas Sowell and decide to jump to the right or the left on that basis. Most people make the decision on an intuitive basis. Maybe it's right-brain or left-brain. Maybe it's more how they feel and less how they think. It's often a complement to other more important life choices. Sometimes it's greed. Sometimes it's duty. At any rate it is too much to be discussed here. What we can discuss are their objectives and their priorities.

When I puzzle over human action or human choice, I tend to revert to lessons I learned in my discipline of economics. All human choices and actions are directed toward fulfilling our dreams within our limits. We want to maximize our happiness, our profits, and our well-being. We want to minimize our pain, our losses, and our discomfort. We are forced to seek these things within limits. The difference between conservatives and liberals is found in the emphasis they place on the objectives or on the limits. Liberals tend to focus on the outcomes and deemphasize or romanticize the limits. They tend to believe the means can be brought to the ends. That is why they like big government in situations where they are not required to produce the means. They deal only with the methods by which the means can be expropriated from others. Conservatives believe this is putting the cart before the horse.

Conservatives place first emphasis on life's limits and how to overcome them. They believe the ends must be brought to the means. Thus they feel a need to put first things first and to ration among competing ends. Conservatives are not romantic. They are pragmatic. They are not dreamers. They are realistic. They measure costs and they know limits. Conservatives value efficiency. That is why they are averse to big government and rely on free markets. Conservatives see an irrefutable connection between ends and means and have a keen understanding of costs and limits. That is why they tend to define the desired results in terms of maximizing output, profits, and returns, while minimizing costs, labor hours, and losses. These objectives are measurable and thus, they are cold, hard facts.

Liberals tend to define desired outcomes in nonempirical, normative terms. They see "New Frontiers" and "Great Societies," a better life, a fairer world, utopian ideals, and higher cultures. They have no operational definition of their goals. They know only that they will know they are there when they get there. In the meantime, it is a noble struggle.

They rarely ask what you know about something. It is impossible to know. They ask how you feel about something. It is far more important to a liberal to have his heart in the right place than to have his head on straight.

Most national discourse on public policy originates with liberals leading with their hearts. With their hearts on their sleeves, they sing in chorus "Wouldn't it be loverly" about the value to someone they love of a new government program. Then comes the conservative with realistic analysis of the potential effectiveness of the program, its alternatives, and its costs, especially in the form of opportunities lost to the chosen option. Of course the conservatives get their brains kicked in because in politics Armey's additional axiom rules: "You can't trump a heart with a brain."

Every person's view of the world and what is possible must be reconciled with that person's occupation. That is why, in the division between doers and thinkers on one hand and dreamers on the other, conservatives tend to be doers and thinkers and liberals tend to be dreamers. It is no accident that people of science, engineering, and commerce tend to be conservative. It is no accident that people of arts and letters, entertainment, and culture tend to be liberals. In the first instance, people tend to the ordinary business of life, and in the second they imitate life. In the first instance the operative question is "What do we have to work with?" In the second instance the operative assertion is "Let's pretend." In the first instance, the intellectual effort and the labor are devoted to getting it done. In the second instance, the energy is in telling the story. Since liberals measure no costs, they have little patience with those who do. They are summarily intolerant of those who speak of limitations. They see them as foot draggers. Conservatives, on the other hand, are impatient and confused by the liberal's seeming inability to see limitations.

It is more fun to be a liberal than a conservative. Liberals party with movie stars and dream big dreams. Conservatives party with CPAs and count the beans. We might all be better off and get along better if liberals would try harder to recognize facts and if conservatives would try harder to be in touch with their feelings. Then maybe we could all party together and have a good time.

———————— ⚜ ————————

If you insist on center stage, you get the tomatoes

———————— ⚜ ————————

This axiom was created for Newt Gingrich. Newt loved being the center of attention and at the front of the class. Newt's motto was "Import ideas, export work," and he loved to build on that. He had an uncanny ability to make the ideas he imported his own and to draw attention to himself while they were being worked out by others to whom he delegated the work. Consequently, while others toiled in relative obscurity, Newt ended up as the public spokesman to the press. When the ideas worked out and were considered sound, Newt shined. When they did not work out or were considered to be quaint, he took a lot of heat. As much as Newt enjoyed the flattering attention, the slings and arrows of critics and ridicule hurt him. Newt was never as hard, callous, or ruthless as he was made out to be by his critics. In fact, he was a gentle soul who longed for approval and appreciation. The harsh misrepresentations made of him were a constant source of sorrow.

I had the opportunity to watch Newt at his most

grandiose and at his most humble. In both cases, Newt was bigger than life and hyperbole was the rule of the day. He could both shout "Hooray" and lament "Alas" in larger tones than anyone I knew. Newt's good news is that he is an historical figure, and history will remember his successes better and longer than his follies. Good for him. He deserves it. But during the time he was the first Republican Speaker in forty years, his highs were his enemy and his lows were his torment. When he was up, he was his own worst enemy. He would become so enthusiastic that he was bound to overreach and take a fall. During those times, I used to quote Waylon Jennings about how whenever he took a fall it was just after he knew it all. Newt's enthusiasm was beyond containment. When he was up, he was bound to press the point, to build on it, and to strike while the iron was hot. That was when he overreached and shot himself in the foot. His critics, I'm convinced, just waited for the overreach, knowing that it would come and that they would enjoy the reversal of Newt's fortunes. They were ruthless, and they always brought it back with a vengeance.

Newt did get a lot of favorable press, and it tickled him. Why not? He certainly earned it! But, even in his favorable press, he took the tomatoes. When *Time* magazine made him the Man of the Year, they used the most unflattering photo imaginable for their cover. When their liberal allies lamented their choice, they were quick to point out the other unsavory characters in history who had been previously selected. After all, Hitler had been, as had Stalin and Nixon. They then soon followed up with "How the Gingrich Stole Christmas" and other barbs to compensate for the disappointment of having earlier "honored" him by grudgingly making him Man of the Year. After all, the press does have standards. Indeed, it has two standards: one for liberals that involves a mile of slack and a ton of luck and one for conservatives that involves no slack and no luck. While they will not live up to a single professional standard of objectivity, they meet this double standard with rigor and devotion.

Newt's most famous gaffe was the time he complained about being forced to exit from the back of Air Force One. This was portrayed as petty childishness on his part. But there is more to the story. President Clinton and several other American dignitaries, including Senator Robert Dole and Speaker Gingrich, had taken Air Force One to Israel for a state funeral. Upon their return, Newt and Senator Dole were told to exit the rear of the plane while President Clinton and other Democrats exited the front to all the cameras and coverage. This was a slight and one not uncommon in the Clinton administration. Newt reacted, not on his own behalf but on behalf of Senator Dole. To Newt, Senator Dole was the head of the Republican party, the majority leader of the United States Senate, and his party's nominee for president. Proper protocol would have dictated that the senator exit the front of the plane with the president. The whole affair was first and foremost a callous breach of protocol by the president or his staff. Dole had enough political savvy to resist the temptation to make a scene and trust to others to point out the obvious breach of protocol and good manners.

Unfortunately, Newt chose not to trust it to luck or to the press's double standard. He spoke right up and registered his complaint. Of course, the predictable happened. The press reported Newt's lamentations as if they were for himself, and the Democrats echoed these reports with enthusiasm. "Crybaby Newt" was the headline we watched gleefully displayed in the well of the House all the next week. Editorials and op-eds rained on Newt. All hope was lost in the effort to set the record straight. Newt as victim of White House rudeness was transformed into Newt the Crybaby. Clinton as boorish perpetrator of errant protocol and rudeness was transformed into the "long-suffering Ashley Wilkes." Even Senator Dole, on behalf of whom Newt had spoken up, distanced himself from the Speaker. During that next week, in the senator's office when the photographers came in for a "photo op," Senator Dole actually got out of his chair and moved to another one in order to avoid being in the picture with Newt. Newt was center stage. The tomatoes were coming. And, he was finding out that "one is the loneliest number in the world." I took that empty seat, and I am glad I did.

While I understood what Newt was trying to do, and I felt bad for him because of the abuse he was taking, I, too, was upset with him for speaking out. He had been around. He knew the press. He should have known that the press was not interested in reporting a Democrat slight of Republicans. He should have known the press would turn it into a negative story about him. His press guy, Tony Blankley, knew it and had warned him to keep it to himself. Newt should have listened to him.

Early in our majority Newt was full of a sense of power and convinced that he could "bring the Democrats and President Clinton to their milk" on the budget. He had seen a government shutdown with the Democrats in the majority and Ronald Reagan in the White House. He knew that the shutdown had been perpetrated by the Democrats and blamed on the president. Without considering the greater likelihood that that scenario was largely due to the press being on the side of the Democrats, Newt concluded that presidents get blamed for shutdowns. By design, Newt and John Kasich, chairman of the Budget Committee, spent the entire summer of 1995 talking about how they would "shut down the government" if the president did not come to an agreement with them about spending. This was before we understood that the press's definition of bipartisan involved Republicans conceding to Democrats. Newt and John thought that the threat of a government shutdown and the likelihood that he would be blamed for it would make the president compliant. So, they decided to make the threat often and clearly.

On the advice of my press guy Eddie Gillespie, I took a different tack. Whenever I was asked about the possibility of a shutdown, couched by the press as a "train wreck," I declared that it was not inevitable, not even likely, and that I did not expect it to happen. That resulted in my not being in the story. I never got to center stage. When the shutdown came, it was President Clinton who did it. It was blamed on the House Republicans in general and Gingrich-Kasich in particular. They got the tomatoes and I did not. They had been center stage and I had not.

Newt took a lot of heat while he was Speaker because of the constant pummeling he took in the press. However, he did draw the fire to his bunker, and that made it possible for most of the rest of us to work without distraction. All too soon he moved on and out of public life. I, then, inherited the mantle of favorite whipping boy for the Democrats and their allies in the press. It has been my role to take the blows while others have been off the hook. Now I am gone from public life, and the heat will be transferred to Tom DeLay without delay. Someone will get the tomatoes. I'm glad it will no longer be me. Nevertheless, I now know what Newt meant when he said, "They never printed the smart things I said." They never do. Not for Republicans.

---- ⚜ ----

Conservatives believe it when they see it, liberals see it when they believe it

---- ⚜ ----

One big difference between conservatives and liberals is in how they see the world. Conservatives see eternal verities. They see rights and wrongs. Words have objective meaning. Facts are facts. Actions have predictable consequences. Life has limits, and reality must be taken as it is. To liberals all things are relative and situational. Even words have no objective meaning to liberals. Any given word, at any given time, may have the meaning ascribed to it by either the speaker or the listener, whichever is more convenient to a liberal purpose. For liberals words have subjective meaning. That is why they think "Depends on what the meaning of the word *is* is" is an answer. They never let the facts get in the way of a good argument. Conservatives are determined to create a new reality, while liberals focus on the impression of reality.

Conservatives are a stubborn bunch. They want to know how you know something. They want to know by how much. They want to see it work. In fact, they won't believe it until they see it. When they see something work like, say, supply-side economics, they stick with it. However, they do require convincing evidence and rigorous responsible analysis. Liberals eschew science. They prefer scenario. They draw their conclusions and then find the facts to fit. That way they can see it when they believe it. Liberals create think tanks to provide evidence that fits their conclusions. My favorite is Citizens for Tax Justice. CTJ is exclusively funded by organized labor and has consistently concluded over the years that all tax cuts benefit the rich and harm the economy. Similarly, they conclude that all tax increases fall on people who "do not pay their fair share" and tax cuts never benefit the economy. Their analytical methods would embarrass the average college freshman in an economics or finance course, but this organization serves the political left well and it is good enough to be taken seriously by much of the press, with its painfully low standards of objectivity.

I once heard my good friend liberal congressman Joe Kennedy of Massachusetts remark: "I have examined the anecdotal evidence, and I conclude that this program serves the nation well." Now I like Joe Kennedy. He is a good guy and a fisherman. He is not a scientist. Not even a social scientist. Anecdotal evidence might be sufficient for Joe Kennedy, but it is not sufficient to confirm the national effectiveness of a government program. Statistical data might be more useful. The program may have done no harm. Maybe it was good but not as good as some other program might have been. Maybe it actually did harm to more people than it benefited, but Joe had not heard anecdotes from those who were harmed. Since I heard his observation in a committee hearing arranged by the Democrats, it is likely that Joe never heard from the people who paid the freight but got none of the benefits. The chairman had been a long-standing advocate of the program, and I knew he had arranged the testimony to support it. I know because my witness, the distinguished economist Thomas Sowell, who had done an exhaustive empirical study of the program and its low ratio of benefit to cost, was denied an appearance in the hearing. Poor Joe Kennedy. He was convinced of a government program's soundness by selected anecdotes from people who benefited rather than examining the larger body of factual analysis regarding both costs and benefits, which was never put before him.

My first policy fight in Congress was over the idea of comparable worth. The liberals had it in their heads that women were discriminated against in the workplace and that new, more expansive government regulations of wages and salary were needed. There were already laws on the books that required equal pay for equal work, but that was not enough to suit the left. The proponents of comparable worth wanted laws that compelled the more subjective standard of comparable pay for comparable work. That is, of course, the stuff of which lawsuits can be made. The entire case for comparable worth was based on one statistical observation: that the average salary of women was less than that for men. There were many objective reasons for this difference; for example, men tended to work in more dangerous and demanding jobs, men tended to have fewer interruptions in their working life, men tended to enter the workforce earlier and stay longer than women, men stayed with a particular job for longer tenures than women, and there were market differences between different jobs. All of that objective information was shunted aside out of deference to that lone statistic that provided the basis for making a federal case out of it.

Despite the fact that empirical multiple regression analysis verified that the average wage differential between men and women was explained by objective and legitimate world-of-work experiences, the liberals stuck with that one lone statistic. Despite the fact that there was little evidence that women with comparable work experience in the same jobs as men were obtaining less than equal pay for equal work, they remained dedicated to their initial conclusion that women were treated unfairly and the government must intervene. To the left, such is the power of a single, unexamined statistical observation. Only a rigid ideological commitment could have overcome the natural impulse to seek an explanation for the most natural of questions: Why do women have an average salary less than men?

Another example of a perception of reality created by liberals was that of the "child-care crisis in America." The Democrats wanted a federally mandated child-care program. They got together with their friends in the media, and the nation was soon subjected to articles and editorials about the nature of the crisis. This media coverage, in turn, was submitted to Congress in support of child-care legislation. The Democrats held hearings featuring a prominent professor from Harvard who was billed as America's pediatrician. They arranged for him to get several awards and much recognition. Despite the fact that there were many empirical studies showing a national surplus of private professional child-care services, they were ready to write their bill. The facts showed that the nation was replete with private child-care facilities operating at underutilized capacities. The facts further demonstrated that there were many low-income families that would use those services if they had grants to do so. With simple scholarships, the existing facilities could be made available to parents who could not otherwise afford it. Watching them talk around that caused me to realize that what the liberals really wanted was government-provided and government-controlled child care. The illusion of a national child-care crisis was created only to enable them to make the case for government child care. At any rate, that was years ago, and it has all faded into distant memory except for a few of us who were there and who put it to rest when we took control of Congress from the illusion makers.

Conservatives are afraid the public will not understand, liberals are afraid the public will understand

T hroughout all my years in public life, I was bedeviled by the constant anxiety of conservatives and Republicans over our failure to get our message out. This is a constant dilemma for conservatives for a variety of reasons. Chief among them is the limited echo chamber for conservative ideals and principles. Conservatism requires deep thinking and has at its core difficult and uncomfortable lessons. Conservatism is based on personal responsibility and self-sufficiency. It embraces no "poor baby" sentiment and no illusions of victimhood. Therefore, it has no auto-therapeutic appeal. Conservatism requires looking beneath the surface at both costs and benefits. It often sounds harsh and uncaring and is incompatible with the sentiments of most of the nation's press. Consequently, when conservatives see reports of their pronouncements in the press, they are most apt to see them abbreviated, distorted, or out of context. Reading what they are alleged to have said results in the legitimate fear that the public will not understand them and a new resolve to be more reticent. It also results in friends admonishing them to "hush up."

For example, near the end of the 107th Congress, I expressed my wonderment over the fact that Senator Daschle, the majority leader of the Senate, continued to prevent President Bush's homeland security bill from passage. I pointed out that recent news reports detailed al-Qaeda's reorganization. I further suggested that people must wonder why al-Qaeda, that ragtag bunch of terrorists, could reorganize and the United States government could not. I suggested that perhaps it was because al-Qaeda did not have a Senate, which it did not. I then pointed out that they did not have a Senator Daschle with another agenda, meaning the next election. The two problems hanging up the legislation were managerial flexibility for the president with respect to labor relations and liability limitations for homeland security vendors. Senator Daschle wanted not only to deny the president the same flexibility the Senate had given President Clinton in managing the FAA in 1995, but he also wanted to deny President Bush the flexibility in labor relations that every president had had since Carter. I pointed out that the largest federal public employees' labor union was the Democrat party's single most generous campaign contributor. Concerning liability limitations for homeland security vendors, I pointed out that this issue was important to the nation's trial lawyers, who were the Democrat party's largest nonunion contributors.

That *post hoc, ergo propter hoc* explanation of why Senator Daschle was holding up homeland defense might not have been the only explanation, but it was factually correct, and no one was offering an alternative explanation. Instead, members of the senator's staff and the chairman of the national Democrat party, whose job it was to collect money for Democrat campaigns, demanded an apology from me for "comparing

Daschle to al-Qaeda." In fact, I had not *compared* him to al-Qaeda. I had *contrasted* him to them. They could reorganize. He could not. Nevertheless, the press ran with their story replete with an out-of-context replay of my remarks. Soon even those Republicans who had been standing with me at the press conference and who had approved of my remarks at that time began to distance themselves from me. Even Senator Trent Lott said, "I like Dick Armey, but sometimes he says some stupid things." Daschle had an echo chamber. I did not. Because people who agreed with me were afraid the public would not understand, they became reticent or worse.

One of the most difficult problems facing conservatives is repudiation by members of their own party. It is hard to keep Republicans on the same page. It is like herding cats onto a flatbed truck. They do not feel bound by, and will not toe, a party line. Their fear of being misunderstood and identified with extreme ultraconservatives is too great. When the liberals and the press turn up the heat, Republican moderates not only retreat fast from the field of battle, but they do so while repudiating the conservative position in the most aggrieved tones. Thus fear of public misunderstanding results in a liberal echo chamber of Republican voices, and the liberal message is given even more credibility because it is not the liberals who are quoted in the press. It is the "thoughtful" Republicans.

If the conservative officeholder does not feel supported by his moderate colleagues, he often feels even less so from his conservative allies. Conservatives are almost by definition against the government. They want results in the business of dismantling big government, and they do not suffer disappointment well. Consequently, they are often harshly critical when success does not come on their terms. As the House Republican leader, I often felt like a two-tailed dog. Both the conservatives and the moderates accused me of "letting the tail wag the dog." Since our conservative message was not presented with unity, we risked the public's misunderstanding.

Liberals, on the other hand, have reality-based fears that the public *will* understand. That is why they get their message out early and often. Liberals tend to be glib and adept at deconstruction. They are masters of reinterpretation, misrepresentation, and spin. For example, when a high school senior asked me if I thought President Clinton should resign in the aftermath of the public's learning of his sexual peccadilloes in the Oval Office, I said no, I do not call on people to resign. I went on to say that if it were me, I would have been so ashamed that I would have resigned. A reporter from the *Dallas Morning News* was present and undeterred. He reported, "Armey calls upon Clinton to resign." The story hit the wires, and the reporter got a nice feather in his cap. The White House immediately swung into action. By the six o'clock news I watched President Clinton's mouthpiece Paul Begala on the White House lawn declaring: "That is the dumbest thing I've ever heard. If dumb ideas ever go to ten dollars a barrel, I want the drilling rights to Dick Armey's head." That was a pretty good line and it got a lot of play. It did crack me up. Paul is a witty fellow.

No one in the press pressed Begala. What was a dumb idea? Was it that such behavior should have resulted in shame? Was it that such embarrassment should have prompted one to resign? Maybe in a world of cultural, ethical, and moral relativism shame and resignation are dumb ideas. Where I come from, they are not. At any rate if inaccurate reporting or arrogance ever goes to ten dollars a barrel, I want the drilling rights to Paul Begala and the *Dallas Morning News*. A little light might have been shed on the matter if anyone in the press had asked Begala whether he thought such behavior was shameful or whether he would have considered resignation in such circumstances. They, of course, did neither. So, we are left to wonder: Just what would shame Paul Begala or cause him to resign?

Speaking of drilling, I must have hit a nerve. The next Tuesday, at my regular "pen and pad," I faced about thirty reporters. Most of them seemed determined to vindicate Bill Clinton. In those difficult days he overacted his role of perpetrator, as the victim and the press were dedicated enablers. The reporters persistently probed me for some sign of sympathy for the president in his hour of need. I had none to give because I thought what the president had done was wrong, undignified, irresponsible, and far beneath the dignity of his office. They grew tired and frustrated. Finally one of them blurted out in sheer exasperation: "Put yourself in his position." I responded: "I would not be in that position. I would be looking up from a pool of blood listening to my wife ask, 'How do I reload this darn thing?'" Now I had the echo chamber. I, too, was witty. So much so that even the press could not resist printing it. I am told it was pithy, but the people who were "pithed" on did not like it.

The greater the pretension, the greater the hypocrisy

I n that wonderfully entertaining arena of sociopolitical discourse we call "conflict of visions," there is nothing as amusing as the game of "gotcha." To claim a "gotcha," you must catch your opponent in some transgression against contemporary political correctness. The game is played by conservative traditionalists who struggle to keep up and by progressive liberals who make, and constantly revise, the rules. The game's moderator is the press who decides what is newsworthy. There are many transgressions for which one can get caught. These include sexism, racism, homophobia, insensitivity, failing to embrace multiculturalism and diversity, being judgmental, being inflexible and, above all else, hypocrisy. While one can score major points for catching one's opponent in any of these transgressions, one gets a TKO if he catches another in hypocrisy. One can be tagged de facto if one fails to keep up with the constantly changing nomenclature of the game. Only liberals get to decide what the "code words" are and what their true meaning is. They also get to decide which socioeconomic-cultural-political classifications can be tagged. There are penalty points for suggesting that a black American can be racist or that a woman can be sexist. To do so is prima facie evidence of your own racism or sexism.

Not only is beauty skin-deep. So is political correctness. That is why an organization can be celebrated for its diversity and multiculturalism if it has white liberals, male liberals, female liberals, black liberals, Hispanic liberals, Asian liberals, and homosexual liberals. Furthermore, people must think like they ought to. A black conservative is labeled an Uncle Tom, and his point of view is discounted. I remember the black conservative economist Thomas Sowell being rebuffed because "There is nothing about Thomas Sowell's life or experience that qualifies him to speak for black Americans." Not to mention that he grew up black and poor, that he is one of the most renowned researchers in America, or that he has a Ph.D. from the University of Chicago. Never mind that the fellow who disavowed him was more light-complexioned than I am. Thomas Sowell's transgression was that he held positions different from than those demanded of black Americans. It is okay on the left to reject ideas. It is also necessary for their survival. After all, if Sowell is heard, the public might understand.

The gotcha game's double standard is one of its greatest sources of confusion. If it is not understood, it is a major source of penalty points. For example, Harry Belafonte can call Colin Powell a "house slave" and then follow up with no apology while he says it is even truer for Dr. Condoleezza Rice. Representative John Conyers Jr., a Democrat from Michigan, can later validate him without editorial comment from the nation's press. Why can they do that? Because Belafonte and Conyers are both black liberals and because Powell and Rice work for a Republican president. On the other hand, the rules don't allow me to call Representative Conyers a "house slave" for defending and expanding the Davis-Bacon Act, even if it works on behalf of the nation's mostly white labor leaders and even if it was originated by northern white workers trying to prevent black southerners from finding work in the North. Why can't I do that? Because I am a southern white conservative. Rules are rules! Now let us get to the main event, hypocrisy.

Jimmy Swaggart was little known outside his flock of followers until he transgressed. When he did get caught, the moment was seized. Here was one of those "holier than thou preachers" consorting with prostitutes. What hypocrisy! Poor Jimmy. He never before nor ever since has attracted so much attention in popular discourse. His transgressions were reason enough for everyone to pile on and make their point. The feminists were outraged. He was treating women like sex objects. So much for biblical teaching. If he was guilty of sexual misconduct, he must certainly have been stealing the money, too. It seemed like Jimmy was to remain on the spit forever, but help was on the way. Along came Jim and Tammy Faye Bakker.

The Bakkers had been even more obscure than Jimmy Swaggart. But they were better print. Here was this cute little couple worshipping the Lord and raking in the money. But not all was well in Heritage USA Park. The story broke about Jim's dalliance with Jessica Hahn. Jessica was an adult and the church secretary. Tammy Faye was crushed, but she made darn good print. The feminists rose to the occasion. Her husband was a role model in a position of authority, and he exploited that innocent little country girl. That was just the kind of sexist behavior they had been warning against, and he was passing himself off as a man of the cloth. What a choice bit of hypocrisy that was. Surely nothing he had ever professed could be taken seriously now. The story got better: Tammy Faye wore too much makeup. And they did a fair bit of swindling for the money, too. They lived too high on the hog. They had an air-conditioned doghouse. How sweet was that! The condemnation of Jim and Tammy's hypocrisy reached dazzling heights. Even Jimmy Swaggart got into the act. Even after Jim went to prison and apologized profusely, even after Tammy Faye divorced and repudiated him, even after Jessica Hahn became a *Playboy* centerfold and more, poor Jim suffered slings and arrows. Swaggart compounded his hypocrisy by declaring himself to be truly repentant, while Bakker was not. Let's look further at how they all demonstrated the greater the pretension, the greater the hypocrisy.

First, Swaggart pretends to be a holy man while he frequents prostitutes. Then he becomes repentant, more so than others. Then Jim Bakker has a tryst with Jessica Hahn while he pretends to be a loving husband and a man of God. Jessica pretends to be an innocent child until she poses for *Playboy*. Jim and Tammy Faye pretend to be "only in it for the love" while they are living the high life. The nation's feminists pretend to be outraged until President Clinton transgresses with a young intern, and then they become silent. The members of the press pretend to be objective and detached while they report one way on Jimmy and Jim and another on Bill. The rest of us have only our sense of humor to keep us from total disgust.

Speaking of Clinton, why did he get away with it? Why, when he defended his proven misconduct with an intern by saying it wasn't sex because "I did nothing to arouse or gratify her," didn't the feminists get upset and angry? It was partly because he managed to get the nation talking about the legal definition of "sex." It was primarily because he had been so celebrated by the feminists for paying lip service to their issues. It was also because too many people did not focus on the real issue of his misleading Congress, his cabinet (especially the women members who stood up for him), and the American people. When Nixon tried to stonewall, the Republicans would have no part of it. When Clinton tried to stonewall, the Democrats manned the barricades. Too many people thought it was beside the point that he lied to a grand jury. But most important, President Clinton was no hypocrite. Everyone knew him to be a rogue, and he did not pretend otherwise. So, his defenses were "So what?" and "What did you expect?" Also, he had a Senate that had zero tolerance for doing its duty and convicting him. Above all, the feminists protected President Clinton. From Mrs. Clinton to the National Organization for Women, they stood by their man. "If it didn't bother them, why should it bother us?" The feminists are the arbitrators of sexual harassment, and they were playing "stand by your man" while President Clinton was playing "alibi Ike." Who were we to argue with that? We were the guys who had better not even be accused of such things. We were the guys on the "zero tolerance" side of sexual harassment.

Some of the most enthusiastic players in the game of "gotcha" are journalists. Journalists are at their worst when they create stories. We expect them to report the story that happens. It is especially unprofessional when they make a story out of something that did not happen. Let me illustrate this with a story that pops up every year. Since 1990, the law of the land gave members of Congress, along with selected other officials, annual cost-of-living adjustments (COLA) equal to one-half a percentage point less than that which is given to federal employees. In approximately half of the years since 1990, Congress has amended the law and denied itself that cost-of-living adjustment. In every year in which a vote was taken, Congress has voted down its COLA. These are facts readily available to any reporter who covers the House. Yet every year some reporters seem obsessed with making the story something it has never been.

Every year many Hill reporters start their annual feeding frenzy. They begin by seeking out members who might be likely to offer an amendment to stop the "pay increase." When a member says he is not, he is pressed to explain what pressures the leadership has put on him to deter him. Reporters beseech leaders on both sides of the aisle to see what steps they are taking to discipline the members. In years where no vote is taken on the COLA increase, they report that "Congress voted itself a pay increase." They treat Congress's failure to vote away the COLA as if it were a major act of hypocrisy. "Gotcha," they say with smug satisfaction. The fact that the story is factually inaccurate does not deter them.

The congressional COLA story is not in itself important. It would not be of much interest if it were accurately reported. What makes it seem important is the implication of hypocrisy. It is included here because it is so easy to get the facts and so obvious that the facts are ignored in order to have a story where there is none. It is, therefore, a good example of the lack of professional standards in journalism. If they are that bad on little things, how can they be trusted with real news? But there is a greater rub. If we believe that a fair, accurate, and impartial press is imperative for a free nation, and I do, who is to discipline the press? We risk our liberties if we ask the government to police the press. No, a better solution would be for the press to discipline itself. In this regard, I call upon David Broder from the *Washington Post*. David is one of the most intelligent, able, and honest journalists I have ever met. He is a liberal, but he has come to that by intelligent, honest introspection. He knows both sides well, but he chose the left. I respect that. He also works very hard at either ignoring his bias or owning right up to it in the things he writes. Since he is one of the best they have, maybe he and others like him could say to their mostly younger colleagues something like "Kill that story. It's not factually correct and it's beneath the dignity of our profession." How refreshing would that be?

I never voted for a pay increase or even a COLA during my eighteen years in Congress. Yet journalists repeatedly accosted me on that point. They zeroed in on me because I have been equally consistent in my opposition to minimum wage increases. To acknowledge that I have been for no increase in minimum wage and no increase for members of Congress would not have been much of a story. There was a consistency that belied a charge of hypocrisy. So what did they do? They implied that I opposed minimum wage increases while I was supportive of congressional pay increases. Like President Clinton and other accomplished "gotcha" players, these journalists seem to hold to the view that it is better to disarm the truth with distraction than to take a hard look at the facts. In this case, minimum wage increases always destroy job opportunities for the poorest and most unskilled workers. What a sad outcome. How much better would it be if these journalists could only realize that they had just played "gotcha" with the defenseless poor and unskilled rather than the big-shot congressman who had left minimum wage jobs behind a long time ago.

Sometimes in the game of "gotcha" the overeager player can give his opponent a chance for a reversal and bonus points. Thus did Ted Koppel on *Nightline* a few years back when he challenged me about my (alleged) vote on "pay increases." My response turned the tables on him and shut him down on the subject. I said, "Well now, Ted, since you make so much more money talking about what I do than I make doing what I do, maybe you really don't want to get into that." Gotcha!

Armey's Axiom
Number 26

―――――― ✻ ――――――

If you don't weep when you must, you'll weep forever

―――――― ✻ ――――――

I include this axiom as a tribute to my wife. Susan D. Armey is a brilliant person and, after my Lord, the most important influence in my life. She is a professional therapist who has helped me, on more occasions than I can recall, to understand others and myself. Her insightfulness has astounded me. I have learned to rely on it as my early warning system. On those occasions when I have taken her counsel, it has served me well. More often than not, when I found myself in trouble, it was because I did not heed what she had to say concerning either the threat I posed to myself or that I faced from others. Susan practices her discipline in part with a methodology called "family of origin." In that method, clients are encouraged to recall family influences in their lives when they were young and to understand the way they affect current behavior. Using that method, she solved one riddle for me.

From the day we met, I have never been able to control my emotions around Susan. She noticed that small, seemingly insignificant, things would set me off with a lump in my throat and tears in my eyes. She further noticed that I worked hard to choke back those emotions. We analyzed it. Moments involving patriotism, spiritual events, and children seemed to be my undoing. For example, we were at Arlington National Cemetery when they played "Taps." I broke down. One day as we drove down a country road we saw a little boy holding a puppy beside a box of puppies and a sign advertising puppies for sale. I broke down. In church I can't get through hymns without breaking down. I try to contain myself, but I can't. It is embarrassing. It is not very manly. We studied further. She prodded me to talk about it. Finally, she helped me to realize that it was all about my relationship with my father.

My father was a man's man. He was a man of the West. He was born in 1914 on a dirt farm in North Dakota. He had nothing for himself, and he expected nothing for himself. By the time he was sixteen he was out of school and working in the Depression-era Civilian Conservation Corps camps. He earned fifty cents a day and sent half of that home to his family. He had nothing. He worked hard. His life had no time for play and no time for sentiment. I remember him telling me, when times were rough, "Take what you have and do the best you can with it. Don't ask for more because there is no more." That is how he lived. He fought in World War II, where he received a Purple Heart, a marksman's pin, two Bronze Stars, and his corporal's stripes. He received an honorable discharge and came home to Cando, North Dakota, where he had a wife, five children, and an old scoop shovel. From that he built a life and a business. He was a good man.

My father was big, strong, handsome, kind, gentle, and stoic. He made Gary Cooper look like a brilliant conversationalist. He was my hero. I do not recall emotion in my father. With his quiet voice and gentle hand, he trained horses, turning those that other men were afraid to handle into state champions. He was the most matter-of-fact man I ever knew. He raised his children to take life as it came, not complain, pull their own weight, and not to cry. Tears were a waste of water. I do not remember being held or hugged by my father, nor do I remember him ever telling me he loved me. I do remember he gave all he had to give and no child was ever left behind or left out. He was a strict disciplinarian, and we were expected to take our punishment like a man and not to be crying about it. The point is that I was not allowed to cry through all those events in a child's life when crying was appropriate behavior. Furthermore, I was not expected to put up with crying when others did it. I was not taught to "feel your pain." I was taught not to be the cause of it and to help you fix it or get over it. "Don't cry over spilled milk." That was the message. Get it behind you and forget about it. There is still work to be done.

My father died suddenly and tragically. Although I cried at his funeral, I quickly bucked myself up, apologized, and resolved not to do it again. I miss my father every day, but I don't cry about it. The way he died broke my heart, but I don't talk about it. I keep it to myself. That is what men do. I just cry about everything else that I associate with him. If I had only wept when I should have, I wouldn't be weeping today. Susan explained it and that is just one of a thousand reasons why I love her.

———————— ✥ ————————

The idea is bigger than the man

———————— ✥ ————————

The great English economist Alfred Marshall argued that few men had original ideas. To Marshall, genius was synthesis. His argument was that anyone who studied and discussed ideas would have a fragmented wealth of knowledge and that genius lay in synthesizing them into whole concepts and original constructs. Marshall is judged to have been a genius, so his testimony is not to be taken lightly. Many people who have never heard of Alfred Marshall have templates for their daily work cut from his insights. In the world of business, cost accounting, managerial accounting, and capital budgeting are based on the insights of Alfred Marshall. The best of contemporary economics stems from Alfred Marshall. Yet he claimed to have never had an original idea.

In the end it is ideas that move us, not people. We praise the person only for the idea for which he is credited. Most of us realize this, but on occasion people who have been credited with ideas get confused and think the acclaim is for them. The person who wants personal acclaim is often the one most likely to discount his own ideas. "Oh heck! That's nothing. I've got a million of them." It is interesting to watch a person jealous of the attention given an idea for which he thinks he should be credited. He shows a high degree of need, one that is likely to get him into serious trouble. It is far healthier to join in the celebration of the idea and to bask in its reflected glory than to show oneself to be insecure and in need of even more attention. Since I am credited with a few noteworthy ideas, let us look at one as an example.

The most celebrated idea for which I am given credit wasn't solely my idea and it was never fully understood. That was the idea of a base-closing commission to solve the problem of redundant and wasteful military bases. At the time, in 1986, there had been not a single closing or realignment of military bases within the United States for over ten years. Congressman Bill Cohen (later senator and secretary of defense under President Clinton) and Speaker Tip O'Neill had stopped all base closings dead in their tracks. They did so by passing an amendment that required an immediate and full environmental restoration before a base could be closed, thus making it too costly for the military. They did this because presidents had been using base closings as punitive political tools, and members of Congress justifiably resented the practice.

I had come to Washington in 1985 to cut the size of government and reduce government spending. I first tried to pare away at discretionary spending in the appropriations bills, but to little avail. I got on the budget committee and found that it labored under the convention of "continuing services baseline budgets," the assumption that every year's budget must continue all services of the previous year with enough increase to cover the cost of inflation. That notion left no room for cuts, but I had to believe that many government programs could be restructured and have even higher success at less cost by reducing waste. Because I could not be accused of being hostile to its mission, I decided to apply my philosophy to the Pentagon.

I convened my chief of staff, Kerry Knott; my legislative director, David Hobbs; my communications director, Ed Gillespie; my district director, Jean Campbell; and my legislative assistant for defense, Brian Gunderson. I outlined the plan and its objectives, and they agreed that we ought to give it a go. We began a collaboration that resulted in a good synthesis and a winning game plan. We researched the problem to find ways to cut defense spending and improve mission performance. We came up with three ideas. The first was "contracting out" base services. That had enormous potential for saving money, but it had formidable opposition in the person of Alabama's congressman Bill Nichols, the subcommittee chairman, and one of the most popular men in the House. The idea might be bigger than the man but *that* idea wasn't bigger than *that* man in *that* body. Bill was a good guy, and I could not offend him and all his friends over a mission doomed to failure by his very popularity.

The second idea was to reform the Federal Acquisition Requirements (FAR). Reforming FAR would involve cutting red tape in spades. It was awful. It was costly. It drove defense contractors crazy both in the Pentagon and among vendors. But it had a high negative demagoguery coefficient. People like Congresswomen Pat Schroeder from Colorado (now retired) and Barbara Boxer from California (now senator) had made the FAR complex and costly on purpose. It was their way of handling their mistrust of the Pentagon and anyone who supplied it. Another Armey's axiom is "Demagoguery beats data in making public policy," and I knew that was just too high of a malarkey hill to overcome.

The third idea was that of closing and realigning obsolete military bases. The only downside to that idea was that it was generally thought to be impossible. We found no deterrence in that, so we went to work. It is generally argued that the key to untying the Gordian knot that had tied up base closings was the creation of a base-closing commission. Actually the key to the resolution was not a single idea but our synthesis of four ideas. They were as follows: create a bipartisan commission that reported to the president, require the president to take all or nothing of what the commission recommended, allow the commission to set aside O'Neill-Cohen, and allow Congress to vote to reject the commission's proposals. The genius of that synthesis was that it allowed Congress to participate but did not allow the president to capriciously target individual congressmen in the manner of the much-resented historical political reprisals.

We made passage of base closing possible through my hard work in hand-to-hand persuasion of my colleagues, pursuant to the legislative game plan constructed by Kerry Knott and David Hobbs and by frequent endorsement of the commission idea on editorial pages all across America pursuant to Eddie Gillespie's excellent press plan. The *New York Times* not only endorsed the idea but also demanded its passage on several occasions. When I first tried to place an editorial outlining the idea, I knew it was big. Since I was not big, I convinced Barry Goldwater to coauthor it. The *New York Times* accepted the Goldwater-Armey editorial. Eddie and I then shopped that editorial and the *New York Times* editorial endorsement to papers all over the country. Their consistent editorial endorsement made enactment of the commission possible. The endorsements were for the *idea*. They were not endorsements of me. I don't kid myself. Newspapers liked the idea in spite of what they thought of me. The idea was bigger than the man.

That base-closing synthesis was not mine alone. It came from all of us working together. The others knew it but, to this day, have never claimed it. I knew it, and to this day I have never convinced Brian, Kerry, David, Jean, and Ed to lay claim to their part of it. They have all chosen, instead, to hold to the ethic that a congressman's staff is the congressman. President Reagan knew it was collaboration and synthesis because I told him so when he signed it. Now you know it, and I feel better about it. I never needed it to be my idea. It was bigger than me.

Although base closing, or BRAC as it is known, is much celebrated and discussed frequently by congressmen and pundits, few have ever digested its reason for being. It was meant to be an example of how everyone could participate in the business of cost cutting. The lesson here is not to let an idea become so big that it eclipses the objective that made it good in the first place.

Armey's Axiom
Number 28

―――――― ✿ ――――――

No man can ever lose his daddy's spurs

―――――― ✿ ――――――

I have mentioned that my father was a man of the West and an extraordinary horseman. While he was not a wealthy man, he left me a precious legacy. Most important, he was an excellent example of how to be a man, a husband, and a father. After he died, a combination of my bad judgment, necessity, and some bad luck resulted in my being left with none of my father's earthly possessions other than his spurs. For the past eighteen years they have been framed and on display in my congressional office. I have never worn those spurs. It would have been a pretension for me to have worn them. They represent his manhood and his accomplishment, which were not my own. I can ride, but not like him. I can train animals, but not like him. I have my own spurs. They are less worn and represent less accomplishment in the horse business than my father's. But, still, of all my father's possessions that came to me, the only ones I did not lose were his spurs. That fact has caused me to see them in a larger perspective.

To the uninitiated, spurs are seen as instruments either to compel a horse to run, which they sometimes are, or to punish the horse, which they should never be. When one learns the proper use of a spur, one learns a valuable lesson in the difference between punishment and discipline. If one takes the time to love and teach, one can discipline and achieve good results. Without the loving and teaching there is only punishment, and that results in more harm than good.

Allow me to digress with two of my father's favorite spur stories: My dad loved the old characters he met hanging around with cowboys. One such old cowboy fascinated him because he wore only one spur. Finally Dad asked him, "Why do you only wear one spur?" "Well, I'll tell you, Glenn, if I can get the right side running, the left side will follow." There may or may not be a lesson there, but it cracks me up. On another occasion my father came across a cussing and screaming man who was punishing his horse so severely by ramming him with his spurs that the poor thing's flanks were bloody. It was so bad that my dad had to intervene. When the old boy responded by saying the horse was no darn good, my dad bought the horse on the spot for two hundred dollars. He started from that moment to love and teach the horse, and we ended up with a mighty fine little cowpony. The horse's name was Jasper, and to this day I love the memory of that good horse.

On the heels of a good horseman, spurs are instruments of teaching, direction, correction, and encouragement. The test of effective spurring is in how gently they are used. They do not need to be sharp and heavy to be effective. On the contrary, they might be most effective when they are rounded off so as to inflict little harm. There is a notion that one must break a horse by "riding him down," that the horse must be manhandled and taught to submit. What gets broken is the horse's spirit. If you want a subject that will cower to your command with little energy or initiative, break him. If you want a partner who will share in the joy of working or playing with you, teach him, love him, and train him.

A good horseman will use his spurs, just as he does his reins and even his weight in the saddle, as instruments of instruction and direction. It is all quite subtle when employed with a well-trained horse that has had the benefit of long association and consistent application of patient and gentle training. It all goes like clockwork when man and horse work together with each knowing the other will be consistent. The results can be marvelous. Man and horse can and often do, love each other. Gene Autry probably meant it when he sang that no woman could break his heart as long as he owned his horse.

There are also, among the uninitiated, those who think you shouldn't use spurs at all. They have the idea that the use of spurs is not humane. Sometimes they are just indifferent to how the horse turns out. It is one thing to think spurs are inhumane and use another technique to train the horse. However, it is quite another to simply do nothing that will effectively teach the animal. Doing nothing is *neglect*. And, neglect is a dangerous game to play. Loving discipline is necessary for proper development, whether it be with children or with horses. That gets me back to the point.

My father's spurs represent to me my father's way of parenting. I was lucky. Dad treated me as well as he treated his horses. He was gentle yet firm. He was consistent in discipline, but I never felt punished by him. He was neither profane nor loud. He did not raise a hand to me, and he was consistent. I knew what was expected, and while he did not literally use spurs to remind and encourage me, this man could get the point across with a few words, a wink, a nod, or a stern look. Each "spurred" me on to do what I could to please him because I loved him. All the lessons of life that he so carefully taught are with me today because they were taught with consistency all the years of my life. I like to believe I wear his spurs (figuratively) with my children, but I know I have not lost them in my life.

I have known others whose fathers wore no spurs, and they have grown up to have undisciplined lives that seem to lack direction and consistency. They seem to "ad hoc" their way along with no plan, no eternal truths, no consistent rules of personal conduct and no way of knowing how it will all turn out. I have known others whose fathers used spurs as sharp instruments of punishment to break them and force them into compliance, and their lives reflect it as well. In the end "No man can lose his father's spurs." We are, more than we know, what we were made to be by our daddy's spurs.

———— ⚜ ————

It's better to be a pleasant surprise than a bitter disappointment

———— ⚜ ————

When we begin any new venture, we place ourselves in a position to be evaluated. This is true for romance, work, and politics. In all such cases it is better to underpromise and overperform than to overpromise and underperform. My wife first taught me this lesson. When I met Susan, she seemed perfect in every way. She was beautiful. She was smarter than she was pretty. And she was nicer than she was smart. She could cook. She kept house beautifully. She was an accomplished professional person. And she was a wonderful mother. I had her on a pedestal, and she pleaded for me to take her off it. She did not want the pressure of living up to my great expectations, and she did not want me to be disenchanted when I got over my infatuation and began to see her shortcomings. In fact, I'm still waiting to see them, but she was very wise. With all her promise, she did not want to overpromise.

It is not all bad to be underestimated. When you are, even competent performance is taken as a pleasant surprise.

By contrast, if one is overestimated, mere competency might result in bitter disappointment. The point is, don't oversell yourself. You might just raise expectations beyond your ability. Promise to do the best you can, and do it. Do not promise how things will turn out. If they turn out better than the expectations you create, you will be a pleasant surprise. If, on the other hand, you overpromise or overbill yourself, it will be hard to live up to those expectations.

Ronald Reagan was a pleasant surprise. He was understated, and that, in turn, was a good complement to the low expectations held of him by all the "experts." The same seems to be true for George W. Bush. Newt Gingrich was a bitter disappointment because he always made such grandiose promises. President Clinton was a bitter disappointment because the "experts" hyped him so greatly. Speaker Dennis Hastert has been a pleasant surprise, except for those of us who have known him over the years. As my brother Charley Armey, general manager of the St. Louis Rams, points out: First-round draft choices often disappoint us, and undrafted free agents are often rare finds.

———————— ✵ ————————

Your worst enemies are your best friends

———————— ⤙ ————————

How many times have we heard it, or for that matter, said it: *"With friends like that, who needs enemies?"* This expression of disappointment invites reflection, because it is heard all too often. We expect our friends to be our friends and our enemies to be our enemies, but sometimes we find that we cannot always count on our friends.

It is not upsetting when enemies play out their expected roles. For years I marveled at reporters who expected me to be upset when Democrats criticized me or my party. To my way of thinking, that was their job—just as it was my job to be critical of them. So what was the big deal? Nevertheless, I was often expected by reporters to react or to give rejoinders. I often frustrated the press when my only response to criticism from Democrats was, "That's their job." I saw no reason to take it personally when the other side objected to me. That was exactly what I should have expected from them. They were only, as Annie Oakley sang, "doing what comes naturally." On the other hand, when my "friends" turned on me, it hurt, and I did take it personally because I had earned the right to expect better treatment from them.

In politics, a rough and tumble business, we especially need for our friends to be steady and reliable. For many it is a blood sport, and well it should be, because the stakes can be very high. So when our friends disappoint us, it is easy to feel abandoned. In 1997 and 1998, I came under a heavy and constant barrage of fire from my "friends." To this day, the only explanation I can find for this assault was that I stood in the way of personal ambitions held by a small handful of "friends" who had somehow managed to recruit others to their efforts. The great shame of it all was that there was a small group of people who had the extraordinary privilege of being in the heights of our government and they were willing to waste it on "office politics" concerning their place in the "firm." Be that as it may, they wanted me out of my position as House majority leader, and they were unrelenting in their efforts to remove me.

Because I did not know why they were attacking me, it was an especially difficult thing to manage. I was confused and hurt. These were my friends. We had been in the wars together. I had counted on them, and they had counted on me. I had every right to expect them to be watching my back, not stabbing it. The worst part was that of all the people with whom I had worked, they had been the most pious and I had thought of them as my most trusted allies. They were my best friends, and because they were, they were my worst enemies. Their criticism mattered because I had cared for them, respected them, and represented them. Unlike the Democrats and their allies, I did not see it as their job to assail me. I couldn't just shrug off the assault as "business as usual," like I had done when my enemies attacked me. This was not "water off a duck's back." It was my world turning upside down.

That experience changed me. It sapped my energy and depressed me in a way that no attack from the other side could have done. I remember retreating into the defensive strategy of not giving a darn when I told my wife: "Honey, I'm just not tough enough to have 'friends' for friends." Still, the experience had its upside. There were those true friends who rallied to my support. There were some among them who put themselves at risk to stand with me. Some of them were harmed for their loyalty. I am very grateful for them. They gave me a new measure of true friendship. They were just as reliable when they were for me as the others were when they were against me.

True friends who stand by you when conspirators move against you are to be treasured not only for their loyalty but also for their courage. When you deal with a true friend, you both deal on the square. When you deal with a false friend, he goes to double-dealing. Double-dealers are almost always vindictive and eager to exact reprisals. That is why the coward gets on the side of the double-dealer. He knows the square shooter will not turn on him with vengeance in his heart, and he is rightly afraid of reprisals from the false friend. The real courage is found in the friend who stands by an innocent victim of a conspiracy, accepts the risk of vendetta, and defends himself only with the truth. That is why we should all remember Armey's additional axiom: "A friend indeed is a friend in need."

———————— ⚜ ————————

The wise hen doesn't cackle until the egg is laid

———————— ⚜ ————————

F ew things in life are as difficult to contain as the anticipation of an impending victory. Bad news always
comes too soon, and good news seems to wait forever.
Consequently, the anticipation of good news tends to give rise
to premature celebration and that, in turn, can result in devastating disappointments. What is more painful than crowing
one minute and eating crow the next? This is often clearly
demonstrated on our playing fields. How many times does
the first-half blowout turn into a second-half comeback? Yogi
Berra must have seen it enough times because he wryly com-
mented: "It ain't over 'til it's over."

The tendency to prematurely celebrate hoped-for good
news or, for that matter, to prematurely bemoan expected bad
news affects the ordinary business of life in the most mundane
ways. How often do we become excited about some terrific
thing we expect to occur and run home to tell our spouse or
the children? "Honey, I'm going to get that promotion." "We
are going to get that new house." "We are all going to Disney

World." These are all great expectations and good news eagerly shared by one's spouse or children or with friends, family, and neighbors. When something unexpected makes it impossible after your wife and children have told all their friends and spent weeks preparing, the disappointment can be devastating. How many times have we promised to do something, raised expectations, and then failed to get it done? How many times have we jumped to a conclusion or lived with a dread fear that was not real? Most times it doesn't matter much except for the embarrassment and the hurt feelings, but sometimes it can matter a whole lot. I remember just such a time in 1987.

Congressman Jim Wright had just been elected Speaker of the United States House of Representatives. He submitted his first budget featuring tax increases and brought it to the House floor. In a legislative body it is a matter of enormous consequence for a new Speaker to pass his first budget. Speaker Wright's stature was on the line, and the tax increase was an ideological benchmark for his party and for his leadership. At that time, there was still a sizable cadre of mostly southern, "yellow-dog" Democrats who were conservative and opposed tax increases. The debate was intense, and the suspense was high. Throughout the entire day there was frantic lobbying on both sides for every possible vote. It was a day of great drama and high stakes. There was enormous tension and tempers were on edge. Nevertheless, the yellow dogs went out on a limb on a close vote and joined with the Republicans not only to defeat the Speaker's budget but also to substitute the Republican budget.

Immediately after the vote was taken, Newt Gingrich went to the well of the House just below the Speaker's dais and gave a short cutting speech, which amounted to rubbing the Speaker's nose in his loss. Speaker Wright just stood there and fumed. But Newt's crowing was more than the yellow dogs were prepared to allow. Their leader grabbed the mike and announced that Newt's words were the most harmful thing he could have done at that moment. Jim Wright saw his moment and seized it. He recessed the House subject to the call of the chair. While the Republicans celebrated, thinking they had stymied the Speaker, he reconvened the Rules Committee and had them report out a new rule to allow the House to reconsider his budget. He then opened renewed negotiations with the yellow dogs. Most of the Republicans spent that time celebrating their victory and congratulating each other. They were enjoying what they thought was the Speaker's abject despair. Speaker Wright was spending his time getting the job done.

After an hour passed, the Speaker reconvened the House, and the Rules Committee reported a new budget rule to be taken up on the next "legislative day." Then the chairman of the Rules Committee moved that the House adjourn to reconvene in thirty minutes. By then the Republicans knew something was up and began to protest. The vote on adjournment was taken, and it passed. Thirty minutes later the House convened for a new "legislative day." The Democrats passed the previous "legislative day's" rule and, subsequently, passed the Speaker's budget. The moral of the story is that sometimes a wise hen doesn't even cackle when the egg is laid, because as Scarlett O'Hara might have said: "Today is a new day."

—————— ⚜ ——————

You can't hunt with the big dogs dressed like a bone

—————— ⚜ ——————

This axiom is fun for the image it conjures. Let's look at it literally. How you dress matters. As they say, "Clothes make the man." Wherever you are, whatever you do, there is a dress code. There are expectations about how you will dress and the appropriate appearance. Sometimes the dress requirements are functional, and more often they are ceremonial, but your compliance with them will influence your effectiveness and acceptance in the group or on the job. It may be fun to be eccentric and nonconforming, but if you insist on your right to be that way, you must be prepared for rejection. Consequently, when the firm publishes its guidelines for dress on "casual Friday," it is a good idea to conform. If everyone wears a suit and tie, you might want to do the same. If an occasion is black-tie, it's black-tie. You can go in a business suit only if you can stand the rejection. Or if you think you are good enough or big enough to "hunt with the big dogs dressed like a bone." If the sign says: "No shirt, no shoes, no service," don't expect to eat with bare feet or a bare chest.

Ronald Reagan never entered the Oval Office without

wearing a suit. For him it was a matter of respect. Many of us found that self-imposed dress code endearing. We thought of it then and cite it now as a measure of the man. The House of Representatives and the Senate require a coat and tie to be worn on their floors. It is a matter of respect. I once saw Speaker O'Neill discipline a member of the House for not wearing a tie while on the floor. It should happen more often when members are improperly dressed, but more importantly, it should never be necessary.

Taking the point figuratively allows us to check our demeanor, our grammar, and our disposition. We should not act like an oaf or sit around scowling and expect a warm reception. But acting refined and being of pleasant nature is not enough. We can betray ourselves with poor grammar. My favorite hockey announcer had this terrible habit of saying things like "he should have went" or "it could have went." Other than that he was outstanding. The man painted vivid word pictures and enhanced my enjoyment of the game. He was a big-time announcer except for his bad grammar. It was such a distraction. Finally, I sent him an e-mail and admonished him for his incorrect usage. He bought it, and now he is hunting with the big dogs with no appearance of a bone.

As we move through life's stages and change venues, we sometime lose sight of the fact that we might need to take some time to review the situation and "brush up our Shakespeare" in order to move from where we have been to where we want to go. The skills and demeanors that serve us well in one setting might not do so well in another. Imagine, for example, how I felt after twenty years as a successful economics professor to discover that members of Congress did not want to hear my lectures on the House floor. It took me a couple of rejections to get the point, but I was much happier and more successful after I did. So were the other members.

Armey's Axiom
Number 33

———— ※ ————

Ninety percent of all talk is unnecessary

———— ⍀ ————

Don't speak unless you can improve on silence.

—SENATOR EDMUND S. MUSKIE

P eople talk too darn much and say too darn little. We go on and on and on, and it's mostly all blather. For example, Howard Cosell was a much-celebrated sports analyst. He was considered to be "articulate." In fact, he was verbose. Instead of saying, "He drops the ball a lot," Cosell would say, "He has a propensity to fumble the proverbial pigskin." Sometimes he would take an important point and make it meaningless by saying too much. For example, "He rushes for an average of 4.5 yards *every time he carries the ball.*" To many sports fans, Cosell diminished our enjoyment of the game because he talked too much. And he must have driven statisticians crazy!

Harry Truman once threatened Congress with the possibility of bringing them back for a special session in July. In July? What was that all about? In those days Congress completed its work before July of each year. Back then they did not have television. They had this wonderful habit of "putting it in the record" instead of standing on the floor and talking all day. Today, with C-Span, there are endless hours of debate that never changes any votes but allows congressmen to show on television how hard they are working. Now, C-Span is wonderful, not because floor debates are scintillating but because of its related programming. There is a lot of truth to that old observation "Congress on the floor is Congress at play. Congress in the committee room is Congress at work." Still, because of C-Span, days, weeks, and months spent legislating are all longer. Even after the House has completed its legislative work, each day features one or more shameless congressmen giving "special orders" talking to an empty chamber for up to an hour on any subject of their choice. In these not so "special orders" they generally play out their political diatribes before the nation. Sometimes they just strut their stuff. We once had an hour on famous redheads in American history by a redheaded congressman.

The need to talk too much is just as bad on talk radio and televised talk shows where the pundits sit around and speculate about what might be our homeland security threat or how we feel about it. We hear endless hours on the extent to which Hillary was properly attentive to the State of the Union Address. During the Democrat presidential primary we will hear speculation about how Tom feels when he sees Dick disagree with Harry. Most of what we hear is made up. For some reason we believe that something is being done if someone is having "a dialogue" about it and "articulating" a position. On most talk shows, there are very few facts. It is nearly all opinion, and for the life of me I have never understood what makes one man's opinion better than another's, except that I might agree with it.

Today there is a "science of talk," and like Gresham's law in economics, bad talk drives out good talk. Verbosity and redundancy are the rules of the day, and no one seems to understand the first rule of brevity. If you know what you are talking about, it only takes a few words. You can go on forever only if you don't know. As Forrest Gump would say, "That's all I have to say about that."

If you are going to go ugly, go ugly early

L ife is full of circumstances that are bound to turn out ugly. Rather than dealing with them, our natural tendency is to procrastinate, deny, and delay. Even when we know that the pain is inevitable but the suffering is optional, we often opt for the suffering. We agonize over it. We try denial. We fantasize that it doesn't really need to be that way, and we wallow in pain and difficulty. In the end we come to the terms that we knew all along were inevitable, but by then we have raised false expectations in others and, like as not, made the situation worse by our delay.

Nobody wants to be the bearer of bad news—the skunk at the garden party. When that sad task falls to us, we naturally try to put it off. How many times have we delayed informing others that we can't really do what is being planned, only to have those others go on with their planning, such that their disappointment is multiplied when we finally do "come clean"? How many times have we rued our delay and bemoaned our failure to face a difficult situation earlier, when it might not have been so bad if we had faced it head-on? These times come to us often in the ordinary business of life, either in the family or on the job. If we do not learn to face up to them, we establish a pattern of delay. We create a lack of trust for ourselves that can become quite painful. Sometimes it can be costly both to our friends and to us. Such a time was 1998 for the Republican majority in the United States House of Representatives.

In 1995, 1996, and 1997 the new Republican majority in the House, under the leadership of Speaker Gingrich and myself as majority leader, and with the reluctant (and sometimes contentious) cooperation of the Appropriations Committee Republicans, did a remarkably good job of holding down growth in government spending. It must be remembered that prior to the Republican majority in 1995, Congress and the nation had experienced, and come to expect, annual increases in spending of some magnitude. So the turnaround had been dramatic. These three consecutive years of success had been difficult, and they had resulted in two irreconcilable expectations for 1998. On one hand, Republican budget cutters expected the new trend to continue. This included most of our Republican voters in America and the majority of the House and the Senate Republicans. On the other hand, the majority of all members of Congress, including some Republicans and most Democrats in both the House and the Senate, all of President Clinton's administration, and a large number of American voters were frustrated in their desire to spend more. This was a perfect scenario for a standoff, and that is exactly what happened for most of the year.

It might be useful to digress for just a moment and explain who the appropriators are in this scenario. Both the House and the Senate have Appropriations Committees, which make the annual decisions about how to spend roughly

30 percent of the government's total budget. That portion of the budget under their jurisdiction is called "discretionary spending," even though for many of us it doesn't seem like much discretion is used regarding it. Individual members of both bodies tend to want very much to be on the Appropriations Committees because it gives them an edge in that time-honored legislative activity known as "bringing home the bacon." The upshot of this is that appropriators are in the business of spending money, and, to them, spending more is generally considered to be better than spending less. Appropriators tend to put their relationship to one another ahead of partisan politics. They tend to work together on a separate "appropriations agenda" and to look after each other. Their sense of unity is so great that it prompted then Senate Majority Leader Trent Lott to remark that "there are really three parties in Congress: the Republicans, the Democrats, and the Appropriators." Finally, the appropriators have one very special circumstance that works in their favor. Congress cannot complete its business and adjourn for the year until all thirteen of their separate appropriations bills are signed into law.

Now back to the story of 1998, which was an election year for the House and a very important one for Republicans. After their losses in 1996, they were concerned about their prospects for maintaining the House majority. It was also important to Speaker Gingrich that it turn out well, given his waning popularity among House Republicans and allied political groups. As the year began, it was painfully clear to both the Speaker and myself that we were headed for an impasse on spending. The Appropriations chairman, Bob Livingston, made it clear that he had had enough of what he thought was my "heavy-handed" restraint on his committee's spending. The Speaker acquiesced to Livingston's demand that he not work with me any longer. That left the ball in the

Speaker's court, and he was not as good at saying no as I had been. The chairman considered that a good arrangement, and he spent the entire year making deals and campaigning for the job of Speaker. Many of our more moderate, mostly north-eastern, Republicans were under pressure from their constituents to spend more. Of course, the Democrats in Congress and in the Clinton administration wanted more spending. The clear majority of the government wanted to go back to larger increases in spending than they had seen in the previous three years.

In a legislative body, the majority of the majority, even though it is often the minority of the body, sets the agenda. Consequently, we began the year with a budget that promised continued spending restraint. Even though we knew the position to be untenable for the whole year, we knew we could pass the separate spending bills through the House at our lower budget levels and work out increases with the Senate later. The Speaker made many ringing pronouncements of his resolve to "hold the line on spending" during the first eight months of that year, even though he knew that in the end he would accede to spending increases. That resulted in fiscal conservatives digging in their heels with growing expectations that we would hold the line against the big spenders in Washington. We had discussed the option of going ugly early and acceding to the higher spending demands, but the Speaker rejected it on the basis that many legislators would vote for things in October, when they wanted to "get out of town," that they would not vote for in July. It was a good point. In the meantime, we spent the summer hearing how our northeastern Republicans were getting beaten up in their reelection campaigns for our low spending levels. Meanwhile, the appropriators just bided their time. Knowing that "the sun doesn't shine on the same old dog every day," they contented themselves with the knowledge that their day would come and they would get more money.

By October the big spenders had consolidated their position, the November elections were drawing ever closer, and most members wanted to get back home and campaign. Everyone wanted the session to end, but it could not end without resolving the appropriations bills. The Speaker entered negotiations with the Senate and the White House and came out with substantial spending increases that the Speaker called "the price of getting out of town." The bill quickly passed the House and the Senate and was signed into law just before the elections. The Democrats were happy. The Clinton White House was happy. The northeastern moderate Republicans were happy. The appropriators were happy. The budget cutters and the conservative Republican voting base were very unhappy. They were bitterly disappointed and felt betrayed. Their morale caved, and they stayed home from the polls nursing the sentiment that it didn't matter anyway because "there wasn't a nickel's worth of difference between Republicans and Democrats."

Congressional Republicans took a pretty bad beating in the election, and several lost their seats. The size of our narrow majority dwindled, and the appropriators and northeastern Republicans gained a strategic advantage for the next Congress and its budget war. The Appropriations chairman toppled the Speaker and had a short tenure as Speaker-elect before his abrupt retirement. It might have been better to go ugly early, which would have given us time to recover before the elections.

———————— ☘ ————————

Never let your face show how bad they are kicking your rear

———————— ⚜ ————————

Throughout our lives we face, from time to time, adversarial situations. This can begin in early childhood with sibling rivalry, and it carries over to the playground, in school, on the job, in marriage, and, most noticeably, on our playing fields. We are advised when we face a hostile animal to show no fear lest we embolden it even further. It is said that the animal can sense our fear and our hesitancy. Certainly a good poker face is advisable when negotiating or, for that matter, playing poker. Poker reminds us that there are times when we might want to reverse this axiom and not let our faces show how bad we are kicking their rears. Gloating can result in as much harm as whining. There are times when this behavior can make an enormous difference in many lives. I was involved in such an instance in 1995.

The new Republican majority in Congress, led by Speaker Gingrich and Majority Leader Dole, had come to an impasse with President Clinton over the budget. Things had gotten so intense that the president actually shut down a small and insignificant number of government operations. The political and public relations campaign was waged over who would be blamed for the shutdown, and most Republicans feared that the president was winning that war. President Clinton and his team were good at creating their own perception of reality. They had much of the public convinced that we Republicans had shut down the entire government and people would not get their paychecks, Social Security checks, and essential services because of the Republicans. We felt that we were behind in the public relations game big-time, and too many Republicans worried aloud about it in public. I am certain that "deer in the headlights" look on the faces of many congressional Republicans encouraged the White House to take the initiative. At the president's invitation, budget negotiations were begun in the Oval Office at the White House. Of course, meetings with the president of the United States are held at his invitation, and on his turf, which, of course, gives him an enormous advantage.

The participants in the budget negotiations were President Clinton, Vice President Gore, Budget Director Leon Panetta, Senate Majority Leader Robert Dole, Senate Minority Leader Tom Daschle, Speaker Newt Gingrich, Minority Leader Dick Gephardt, and myself as majority leader of the House. We were on their turf, and we were outnumbered five to three. At the outset, the Speaker, in his confidence, thought that made the odds about right. As the talks developed, the principal negotiators were President Clinton and Speaker Gingrich. Vice President Gore and I seemed to play the roles of "political officers," with his restraining President Clinton when he seemed to be giving too much and with my restraining the Speaker when he seemed to be doing the same. Leon Panetta was supposed to play the role of independent advisor and scorekeeper to work out a way for the various pieces to fit together. Majority Leader Dole, who I thought should have asserted more leadership, was the stoic one. For most of the time, he seemed almost indifferent to it all.

The talks lasted through November and right up to Christmas. In fact, I believe I spent more time with President Clinton that Christmas season than I did with my wife. After each session at the White House, Dole, Gingrich, and I would repair to the Capitol and brief our House and Senate Budget Committee chairmen. The Democrats remained at the White House and reviewed the session. But, they also did something more. They briefed the press and they did a good job of putting their spin on the story. We spent the whole time playing catch-up with the press. This was a high-stakes poker game, and it seemed to me that everyone had his game face on. I could detect no break in anyone's nerve for a long time. And then it happened!

After a particularly difficult session, I wearied of the whole thing and suggested we not go back for further meetings. I had come to believe that the president was trifling with us and that he had no intention of bargaining in good faith. Majority Leader Dole and Speaker Gingrich agreed with me. We were in Dole's office discussing the matter when the White House called. It was the president, wanting to know if we were coming over. Dole politely suggested that we might not do so. He pointed out that we had serious doubts about whether it would be worth our time. He was tactful, courteous, and diplomatic. He explained that I was unhappy about the manner in which the White House had used pictures of the meetings, in violation of the president's personal assurance that they would not do so, to spin the story with the press. I felt especially betrayed because I had a long-standing rule against having my picture taken in the Clinton White House. I had agreed to have my picture taken only because the president and the vice president had assured me that the pictures were only for White House archives. Despite my anger and frustration, I discussed it with the president quietly and politely. The Speaker then came to the phone and unleashed all his frustrations in a most profane and angry manner. I was stunned, and Leader Dole was appalled by the tirade. After the White House call, we all agreed that there would be no more meetings over the weekend. I repaired to my place in the country. The Speaker and Majority Leader Dole remained in the senator's office for a personal discussion.

I am not sure what went on during the next two days, but I was subsequently called by the Speaker and informed that he and Majority Leader Dole had come to an agreement with the White House. It was pretty much on White House terms, but I felt that I had no choice but to reluctantly accept it. I have always believed that the Speaker's tirade and Majority Leader Dole's embarrassment over it were the catalysts that resulted in an unsatisfactory outcome for us. Some years later, we all learned that right up to that minute the president had been feeling a growing sense of despair and had come to a point where he was willing to make concessions to us. The difference was that he never let us see that we had him on the ropes.

Old fogies don't tolerate young fogies

When I was a boy, one of the things I was told was that "you have to keep up with the times." I suppose that is clear to everyone, but it can be a hard thing to do, given the dispositions of insecure people who attain leadership positions. For our purposes here, we will call an insecure person a "fogy." Old fogies are often people who have a position and are insecure about being displaced by others. Young fogies are people who are trying to improve their positions. Because they are young, they are often more current with technology and methodology than the old fogies. When young fogies try to make changes while being insensitive to the insecurities of old fogies, they often meet with intolerant resistance. That resistance, in turn, impedes progress.

My first experience with this was in the university during the late 1970s and early 1980s. I had joined a faculty that was light-years behind the times. It was an economics faculty that did no research, practiced a peculiar methodology, neither

had nor used any computerized methods, and did no empirical or quantitative work. It was truly a case of "sleepy time
down South." Despite those shortcomings, the tenured faculty
liked it just the way it was and was loath to change. In fact, the
reason I was hired was that the dean of the business school had
threatened that if they did not "get with the times" he was
going to start his own economics department. That would
have resulted in the loss of about 95 percent of our students.

The legacy faculty managed to tolerate me fairly well as
long as I tended to my own teaching and research and did not
try to force my newfangled ideas on them. I was content to
do so. Eventually I came up for tenure. I had some difficulty
getting excited about tenure since I knew that tenure meant
"not enough money forever." Still, I applied for it since the
alternative was to leave the university, and I was not ready to
uproot my family over such a little matter. I had written several articles, presented several scholarly papers, and written an
advanced text for one of my discipline's more difficult
courses, price theory. Despite the fact that my teaching and
publication record was better than any of the tenured faculty,
they granted me tenure only reluctantly, while seizing the
moment to remind me that they really did not approve of my
kind of economics. Eventually, the dean asked me to chair the
department. That did not sit well with the old fogies. They
saw it as a conspiracy to force them to change their ways and
methods. Nevertheless, I accepted the assignment and immediately went to work updating the department without
expecting them to make personal changes in what they did.
My approach to changing the department without upsetting
their personal applecarts was modeled on the advice of one of
their methodological leaders, John Kenneth Galbraith, who
had written that we should "let the old fogies die off and not

tolerate the young fogies." Of course, Galbraith was writing about economists like me in deference to economists like them.

I installed the department's first computers and began training students in their use. The students were excited. I called an old friend, Mike Ellis, who had been in the department but had left in frustration, to tell him we were beginning a new day and to convince him to come back. He did. Mike was the best teacher of economics I ever knew. He was current on quantitative methods and taught statistics so well that students actually enjoyed his courses. We were lucky to have him back. Over the next few years I hired five additional young faculty, all of whom were methodologically up-to-date, good researchers, and effective teachers. This resulted in a divided department, with young fogies who were less than appreciative of the old fogies who were, in turn, quite intolerant of young fogies. Those were exciting times of internecine warfare.

In 1983 three things happened that tipped the scales back in favor of the old fogies. The dean of the business school, who had insisted on hiring me in the first place, retired and was replaced with an old friend of my old-fogy faculty. The dean of Arts and Sciences who had made me chairman died and was replaced with a fellow who had a Ph.D. from the Duke University English department. I decided to leave the university and run for Congress. One of the old fogies was made department chairman. He and the tenure committee refused tenure to everyone I had hired, despite the fact that each of them had a better publications record than every member of the tenure committee. Soon the department was back to being that same sleepy little department it had been before I came there. Eventually, however, all the old fogies I

ᴀRMEY'S AXIOMS

had known took their retirement, and the university brought
in a new chairman from outside who remade it once again in
the image of what I had been trying to achieve. That goes to
show you that you can't stop progress, but you can slow it
down.

I went on to the United States House of Representatives, where I was promptly told by the "old bulls" to take a
seat on the back bench and not speak until I was spoken to. I
was told to not rock the boat. I didn't listen to them, either.

Don't go back and check on a dead skunk

Willie Nelson has a great song called "There's Nothing I Can Do about It Now." It is full of lamentations about the mistakes he has made and his realization that none of them can be undone, so he just has to go on with the memories. It is a great old song with a good point. The point is to "get over it." Regrets may be inevitable, but wallowing in regret is unnecessary and fruitless. How many times do we have a bad time and then insist on reliving it? We are like criminals who can't resist revisiting the scene of the crime. We obsessively return to it over and over as if somehow we can set things right when we ought to just get on down the road and put it behind us. When you run over a skunk, it is going to leave a terrible smell where you hit it, but if you drive far enough fast enough, you can leave it behind. Still, there is that urge to go back and check on it.

I did that once in a most memorable way. Many years ago I inadvertently mispronounced a colleague's name in a way that enabled him and many other people with the same "orientation" to feign moral outrage on the grounds of my insensitivity and lack of political correctness. In my estimation the whole affair was blown out of proportion, and too much was made of what came to be regarded as my backward and mean-spirited disposition. It was a particular nuisance to me because it concerned a subject in which I was, in fact, quite uninterested. Still, since people often find that it is better to be persecuted than ignored and since it is often comforting in this politically correct world to be the victim, a great many people insisted on citing that split-second mispronunciation as the definition of my character. That is what I call a "bum rap." So I looked for a chance to set the record straight.

Several years later, at the Republican National Convention, I received an invitation from a colleague with the same orientation as those offended to attend a fund-raiser on his behalf at a Philadelphia bar that was quite popular with persons of that orientation. In my naiveté I accepted the invitation and went to the event. This, I thought, would demonstrate that I was an open-minded person of good heart and, perhaps, diminish the bad feelings. Soon after my arrival, my presence was noted, and I was subjected to what I thought was some good-humored razzing. Now, my name is Dick Armey, and that can be the source of some fun jokes and kidding. That is what I thought I was getting. But what the heck, I'm a cool guy. I joined in the fun to show I was a good sport. I retold a joke concerning my name and the originally "offended" colleague that I had heard Jay Leno tell on *The Tonight Show*. Now that joke had been considered quite funny when Leno told it, and since I, too, was the butt of the joke, I was sure my telling it would demonstrate that I was a good-humored guy with no malice in my heart. It didn't turn out that way for me.

Going back to check on that old dead skunk only made me the skunk at their garden party, and they raised a big stink about it. For two days I was the talk of the convention. The same joke that Leno got paid millions to tell was a source of moral outrage when told by me. Even the president was asked to comment on my "intolerant remarks." I would have been better off to leave it alone, as I would, most likely, have been better off leaving it out of this now most controversial chapter of the book.

Armey's Axiom
Number 38

---◆---

If ifs and buts
were candy and nuts,
we would all have
a merry Christmas

---◆---

How many times do we wish things were not as they are? Rather than coming to terms with unpleasant realities, we entertain ourselves with the thought that they're not supposed to be that way. Instead of getting on with life, we wonder "What if?" or we discount the necessity of taking a necessary course of action with our "buts." While such sentiments may be therapeutic, they are of little use in the cold hard business of dealing with the world as it really is. Some things are facts. They may not be pleasant facts, but they are facts. Some things are out of our control, and it simply doesn't matter whether they might have been different. So we must learn to deal with them.

Speaker Gingrich could on occasion face the music quite well. He faced many complex and difficult circumstances during the time he was Speaker, and he had an observation, which he made during those times when he was at his best. Whenever we were sitting around wishing things were different, he would say, "That is a fact, not an option, so let's deal with it." It was always a sobering moment that forced us to get down to brass tacks and get the job done.

My wife's cousin, Keith Gross, gave me this axiom. Keith was always fun. He had a reassuring nonchalance that made you wonder if anything could get him down. He lived by two rules. Rule number one was "Don't sweat the small stuff." Rule number two was "It is all small stuff." He had had a bad accident and was left in a great deal of pain. We were very empathic with him at times and would wonder, "what if" he had not gone to work that day, or "what if" he had taken another route. Sometimes we denied his pain, and we argued "but" it might go away. He would just smile and say, "What's your point, bub? If ifs and buts were candy and nuts, we'd all have a merry Christmas." He died before that Christmas, and we still miss him.

Armey's Axiom
Number 39

—————— ⚜ ——————

There is nothing to be learned from the second kick of a mule

—————— ⚜ ——————

How many times must we make the same mistake and suffer the same consequences before we correct our behavior? How many times do we ignore Jimmy Buffett's good advice when he admonishes us with "You got to learn from the wrong things you done"? Or as Congressman Jim Nussle says: "If you always do what you always did, you will always get what you always got." It reminds me of my favorite definition of *crazy,* which is continuing to do the same thing and expecting a different result. Still, nevertheless, we all have certain behaviors that seem to be habitual and self-destructive, and we all seem to have difficulty in changing the patterns. We all too often repeat a harmful behavior with no explanation other than "The devil made me do it the first time, the second time I did it on my own."

I have always had a chronic aversion to conflict. I will resort to all kinds of rationalization, procrastination, or denial in order to avoid a confrontation. Inevitably, those conflict avoidance mechanisms result in the problem becoming worse rather than better and further complicated because of my appearance of "hiding something." It is a pattern I have repeated with my wife, who always meets problems head-on, to her near total exasperation. Fortunately, she is willing to be patient and work with me, but it has taken me years just to get better. Perhaps it would have been better if she had hit me between the eyes with a two-by-four in order to get my attention. In that case, I might have learned more quickly and made the desirable change in my behavior.

Painful lessons are lessons well learned. If we are required to live with the consequences of our mistakes, we don't forget them. That is why enablers are hurtful. An enabler is someone who sees someone they love making repeated mistakes and responds with too much understanding in a way that shields the person from the consequences. In doing so, the enabler denies critical information to the person making the mistake, and behavior adjustments are not likely to take place. The point is, within reason, let the consequences come as they may, and improvement will follow.

My father understood that well. Once when I was young, I was arrested for alcohol possession. The police had me in custody and called my father. His response was that they should just keep me until they were through with me then send me on home. He had work for me to do. I felt alone and scared sitting in that jailhouse, and when the police sent me home, my father worked me like a borrowed mule. He didn't lecture me. He just left me to figure it all out. I never had that problem again. Many years later, I had the opportunity to repeat the lesson for my oldest son, David, in the same situation. He never had that problem again, either.

———— ⚜ ————

Washington is a city of young idealists and old cynics

———— ⚜ ————

I, like everyone else I have known in Washington, came to the city as a young idealist. Whether liberal or conservative, everyone comes to that town with a vision of the things they want to do for America. They may want more or they may want less big government influence over the ordinary business of American life, but they all want to do something for the country. All kinds of people come to Washington with pockets full of dreams and good intentions. They come to make a difference. They think Washington is a city that serves the nation and they want to be part of it. They are like sheep among wolves. And Washington wants them, too.

The natural tendency for any person in any new venue is to want to fit in, to be accepted, and to be part of the action. Therein lies the seduction. Washington welcomes with open arms. The city is such a place in the sun that people rush to become a part of it while still believing it to be the city of their dreams. If they are not careful, they will fit right in before they understand the city and its self-absorption. The city is involved

---

in an eternal love affair with itself. There is a never-ending supply of cocktail parties, dinners, testimonials, awards, and banquets. There are big shots, media celebrities, and visiting glitterati. It is a city of constant celebration and testimony to the good work that it does. If you listen to Washington on Washington, you wonder why you would want to be anywhere else. And too many young idealists listen too much.

Washington is a city totally obsessed with itself. It is the only city in America that makes its entire living off the rest of the country. The city produces nothing. It only taxes, regulates, spends, and compels through the use of force. But, according to itself, it does these things for the best of all reasons and only because it must. Washington is a city that is obsessed with social stratification, position, status, and, above all, power. It has, as John F. Kennedy said, the charm of the North and the efficiency of the South. Speaking of Kennedy, Washington did not get the message in his most famous quote: This city asks not what it can do for the country. It asks only what it can do for itself.

If you come to Washington as a young idealist and you are happy with who you are and would like to remain so, the trick is not to fit in. My line is: "You had better know who you are before you get there or someone will darn sure own you by sundown." It is a predatory and seductive place that likes to keep people sorted out according to spheres of influence. Who you know can quickly become more important than what you know. It is a place where the sages counsel you to "go along to get along" and to hitch your wagon to a star. You should network, become part of a power base, and work for the good of that order.

The city is a collection of cliques, good-old-boy networks, careerists, private schools, and social clubs. You are either in or you are out, and getting in, should you want to, is hard to do. Presidents, cabinet members, congressmen, and senators are all viewed as interlopers. The city knows that they are not long for that world and that whatever they do to disturb things can be quickly set right as soon as they leave. The nation might have elected the president and found him to be quite desirable, but Washington merely puts up with him until he leaves. Despite the collective judgment of the nation that he is the right guy for the job, Washington reserves its applause until he grows into it. Likewise, a cabinet secretary is a nuisance who only disrupts the mundane routine of the agency. Things will be put back to normal soon enough when he is gone.

The city consoles itself with the knowledge that if some member of Congress or some senator decides to stay for a long tenure they will soon fit in. The senator who buys a home and moves his family into the right school is an object of approval. The congressman who leaves his family back home and sleeps on the couch in his office is suspect. The Washington establishment quickly concludes that his aberrant behavior must be a statement about the city. It is inconceivable to them that it is really about his family wanting to remain at home. So, if you want to fit in, moving to the city is the ticket. Many do, and often they don't go home to America again. They fit in and take their turn at initiating the new people. They grow old in Washington while forgetting where they came from and why they came to the city. They forget their idealism about America and become cynical Washingtonians amused by the naïve newcomers coming to town each year with grandiose plans to serve the country. How quaint!

If you want to come to Washington as a young idealist and leave as an old idealist rather than an old cynic, I have three pieces of advice: First, never let Washington be your home. Keep your home in America where real people make real livings producing real things for real people. Never lose your ability to identify with them and their problems. Second, stay close to the young people with whom you can work. In my case, as a member of the House of Representatives, it was the young staff and the younger members of the House who kept me aware of our reasons for coming there in the first place. Youth doesn't have to be wasted on the young. It can be an encouragement to the old. Third, don't stay too long. You must know when it is time to go, and that time is when what happens in Washington becomes more important to you than what happens in America.

For all its faults, the city can be very generous. It celebrates you when you leave. Washingtonians give you a fine send-off. Makes you wonder why you don't stay. But then, if you are leaving, you probably didn't fit in. Leave early enough, and you can leave an old idealist. That is not a bad trick if you can pull it off. Oh, by the way, it is perfectly consistent with being idealistic about America to be cynical about Washington.